The Reason We Are Here

The Truth

Mary McGovern

A VERAVAIL Book

Requests for permission should be addressed to:
VerAvail
515 E Carefree Hwy #424
Phoenix, AZ 85085
www.TheTruthIsLove.com

ISBN 0-9749224-8-X
Library of Congress Control Number: 2004104986

Cover Design: Graphics by Manjari
Layout: J. L Saloff
Font: Times New Roman, Nat VignetteOne

McGovern, Mary
   The Reason We Are Here – The Truth

First Edition

God does not require you to succeed.
He only requires that you try.
— *Mother Teresa*

Table of Contents

Acknowledgments . . . .*ix*

1 Life's Success? *1*
2 Why Are We Here? *7*

Part 1

3 Clarifications *13*
   The Higher Power, One Divine Source, aka "God" 13
   Eternal Life, the Afterlife *14*
   Mankind *15*
   Levels of Consciousness and Different Life Paths . .*15*
4 Soul-Spirit, Ego-Mind *17*
   The Soul-Spirit *17*
   The Ego-Mind *20*
   Superior Ego *22*
   The Subconscious Mind *23*
   The Body *24*
   Balancing the Physical and the Nonphysical *25*

Part 2

5 The Truth **31**
The Truth Is: *33*
There Is One Divine Source *33*
God's Love Is Unconditional for All Mankind *34*
We Are All Created Equal, We Are All One,
    All Our Souls Are Interconnected *35*
The Soul Is Eternal *37*
The Truth Is Inherent Within Each of Us *38*
The Golden Rule *39*
The Law of Karma *41*
The Values of the Truth *43*
    Love *44*
    Peace *47*
    Integrity *49*
    Humility *49*
    Compassion *50*
    Forgiveness *52*
Faith *55*
6 The Truth of Human Life **57**
The Truth of Human Life Is: *57*
Dealing With the Truth of Human Life *58*
The Gift of Love *58*
The Gift of Human Life *58*
The Gift of Knowledge of the Truth *59*
The Gift of Free Will *60*
Each Life Is a Journey With a Purpose *61*
Change Is Constant, We Are Not in Control,
    and Everything Happens For a Reason *63*
Each of Us Is Responsible for Our Own Life *64*
Each of Us Has Good and Bad Qualities *66*
Life's Wake-Up Calls Are Meant to Get
    Our Attention *68*
Human Life Is Temporary *69*
God's Unconditional Love and Support *71*

Becoming Conscious and Connected to the Truth . . *72*
Reality of the Ego-Based Distortions of the Truth . . *73*
Society and the Truth *74*
We Are Here to Learn *75*
7 Senses of the Soul **77**
The Intuition of Your Soul *77*
The Inherent Knowledge of the Truth *83*
The Innate Hunger for Our Oneness With God *83*

Part 3

8 Religion **87**
Are We Sinners? *93*
Conceived by Immaculate Conception? *95*
The Bible *96*
The Life of Jesus Christ *101*
Religion and Consciousness *104*
9 Spirituality **107**

Part 4

10 Consciousness **115**
11 Self-Esteem, Honoring Yourself **131**
12 Detachment **139**
13 Living in the Present Moment **143**
14 Life Is Fair **149**
The Energy of Our Being *155*
15 Life's Lessons **161**
Thoughts, Emotions, and Feelings *167*
Fear *172*
Judgment and Intolerance *175*
Relationships *180*
Soul Mates *182*
The Learning Process *182*

Part 5

16 Becoming Conscious, The Connection . . .187

Going Within *189*

Quieting Your Mind *191*

Letting Go and Surrender *194*

Living It *197*

Relationship With God *199*

Communicating With God *201*

Part 6

17 It Is Up to Us 207

Background *213*

Acknowledgments

I would like to express appreciation to everyone I have interacted with throughout my life, and those I have yet to meet. Life is about experiences, and it is from our experiences that we learn. We are here to learn together, even if it does not always appear that way.

To my brother Tom, for being a great brother and good friend.

To my companions, Julie, Nikki, Sam, Amanda, Lady, Jack, Kara, Max, Apache, Joe, Susie, and Bailey, for the pleasure they have brought to my life.

I would like to extend a special thanks to Linda McPherson for helping me to realize the title, and for her support and assistance.

I wish to thank Tom Bird for his teaching that validated my experience. To Manjari Henderson, of Graphics by Manjari, for designing the cover. She captured the essences I was looking for. To Jamie Saloff, not only for the formatting and guidance in publishing, but also for all her support, encouragement, and conversation.

I would like to acknowledge Dr. Robert Koppen, M.D. for helping me start this transition in my life. To Gail Minogue, for giving deeper meaning to all things happen for a reason.

I am deeply thankful to Julia Ingram. I will be forever grateful to her for the enhancement she brought to my life. She brought clarity to my spiritual experiences. This book would have lacked depth and meaning without her assistance.

To all the wonderful spiritually advanced individuals that are here at this time making a difference, creating awareness, and adding meaning to our lives.

I want to acknowledge God, Jeshua (Jesus), and Archangel Michael for the roles they have in my life. Words cannot express the effect of their presence. I want to thank Jeshua for his guidance and being by my side, Michael for his support, and God for his guidance and giving me this life path. Without them, this book would not exist.

1

Life's Success?

How often have you wondered what life is really about? Ever wondered why everyone is in such a hurry, so busy – doing what, and why? What is the point of all this craziness we call life? What price are we paying for our complicated lives?

One day, midmorning, I drove into the city. I was on the freeway and then on the city streets. This particular day everyone was rushing about, darting in and out aggressively and often rudely. You could feel a sense of tension within almost everyone. I wondered where everyone was going and what was so stressful and/or important. I was quite sure none of them really knew. This chaos reminded me of the very large anthills out in the desert, where the ants appear to be scurrying about wildly in total disarray. However, there is an order to the ants rushing about. They know where they are going and more importantly they know why. The ants are simply fulfilling their role in life. Unfortunately, many of us do not know where we are going or what our role in life is. We are so busy going, doing, and being involved in "life" that we do not stop long enough to realize our life's real meaning much less what our lives are about. Many are searching for success and satisfaction in life with misguided directions based on worldly values. Have we lost sight of life's real meaning and are we missing the point of what life is really about? For the ants it is easy, they simply follow their instincts. It can be for us as well, if we follow the intuition of our souls.

What is your definition of a successful life? Would you base your definition of success on money, possessions, a career or job, a title or the position you hold, achievements, your lifestyle, a big house, nice cars, the toys, etc? Does success mean living the American Dream? What is the American Dream really? What is your life's dream? What does happiness mean to you? What would it mean to you to live a life of inner peace with true contentment and satisfaction?

We have become a superficial, materialistic, youth-oriented society driven by our egos, and we seem to have lost our prospective and respect for life. We have become a throwaway society that takes so much for granted. We seem to have no real sense of direction or value for what really matters. Mankind has become arrogant and self-serving, which has resulted in us becoming selfless rather than self-confident. Humility, humbleness, and reverence for life are qualities many do not give much thought to or embrace.

We have convinced ourselves that material possessions, winning and being right are more important than doing the right thing, or having peace and contentment. We actually equate finances with our level of contentment and satisfaction in life. The image that money can buy anything and everything seems to be our belief. As a result, what is true has become distorted, and all that seems to matter is the desired outcome.

We are not honest with ourselves about how we feel about our lives, we do not know who we really are, or what we value in life. What we say we value in life is not reflected in how we live our lives. We say we value faith, peace, family, health, happiness, and contentment, but do we really?

Most of us do not want to hear, feel, or face the truth about ourselves or about life in general, and none of us like to deal with our own weaknesses, emotions, and feelings. Yet, deep down, each of us knows what is true about our lives. We would rather life be easy. We want the fairy tale. We have convinced ourselves that truth and honesty hurt. We have also decided that life is not fair. This is because we do not want to take responsibility for our lives.

We look to the material success to bring us the satisfaction and meaning we are searching for. We have become so caught up in the going, doing, and being, that we do not stop long enough to take stock of our lives and to consider what really matters. What we consider successful has caused our lives to become complicated, frustrating, and stressful. We are living this way, but why?

Today's world measures the value of life in terms of money or the appearance of money. Money has become an idol to our culture and the world. We have the idea that bigger is better, more is better, and winning is more important than losing. We want everything now, fast, and instant, from the way we communicate to the food we eat. Money is used to satisfy our selfish wants, needs, and greediness. Money even overrides our treatment of the environment.

We associate wealth with glamour and being able to have it all. True success in life has nothing to do with material possessions or wealth. For example, neither a big, elaborate, expensive wedding, nor a simple, affordable wedding has anything to do the success of the marriage. Money or the lack of it will not create value, respect, or what matters at any level. It will only create the illusion. True value and respect are about who you are as a person and what matters is reflected in *how* you live your life.

Money and the economy seem to run our lives. Even Christmas is more about the effect of the retail sales volume than it is about the reason for the holiday. Our general attitudes and lifestyles have become based on the economy. In a good economy, we are more carefree, positive, and appear to be less stressed. In a bad economy, we are more cautious, negative, agitated, and stressed.

Much of today's lifestyle reflects the illusion that money is the answer. Fortunately, money is not the answer, but money and the acquiring of it is what runs our lives. Money can buy good times and make life appear easier on the surface, but it cannot buy what truly matters in life. Unfortunately, in today's world what money can buy has created the illusion of the haves and the have nots. This has led to the illusions of superiority and inferiority, and has given us an even more distorted illusion of life's value.

Please do not misunderstand that money should be thought of as bad, or that we should all be poor. It is the illusion of what the money means to our lives, the value we give it, and the effect it has on our self-esteem that is the issue. Abundance in life is and can be wonderful. It is even good and satisfying to enjoy the superficial successes and the material stuff that is part of our human lives, as long as the value is kept in perspective. When our focus revolves around only the material aspects of life, we sacrifice who we are, and we do this without even being aware of it. This has resulted in the quality of our lives and the reality of our existence becoming shallow. The goals and achievements in our lives have become about the material success, monetary gain, and feeding our egos. The material successes in life are temporary, and we do not realize this until we are forced to face the reality of our lives.

The richness of life is about who you are on the inside and how you live your life, and this is not a result of being financially rich. A truly happy and satisfying life has nothing to do with whether you are rich or poor. It is important to realize the choice for internal wealth is yours to make, and so is the choice for financial wealth. In this world, all things are possible and with no limits. The only limits are those you set for yourself.

God wants us to live an abundant life. Having it all comes from becoming conscious, being connected with your soul, and living your life authentically. The worldly material possessions are just stuff. No amount of material stuff can make you truly satisfied, happy, and content in life unless you are true to yourself, love yourself, and are connected to your soul. When you are connected to your soul, you create a flow of positive energy for yourself, and abundance in all aspects of your life.

Life's success is not about wealth, power, control, possessions, or achievements. These are all false images of success. Money does not buy love, happiness, security, contentment, inner peace, a sense of self, acceptance, or respect, but we live our lives as if it does. Most of us are very aware of these facts, however being aware of all this has done little to change how we approach life. Life for many, whether we realize it or not, has become similar to puppets dangling on society's superficial strings. Our ego-minds have caused us to become like puppets that are manipulated and influenced by society. Do you feel the need to conform to fit in, when fitting in is really not who you are, or what your life is about? Are you allowing a material life and the material world to control you? To have true success in life, you will need to cut yourself free from society's strings and become a conscious individual.

We are creatures of habit and tribal by nature. A tribal culture requires conformity. Things are done simply because it is the way it has always been done, or it is the way everyone is currently doing it. We need to look and act a certain way to fit in and to keep up with the current trends. Anyone who does not go along is considered odd or different, so being an individual can be difficult. As a result, we get caught up in what we think living life should be. We become what society, our families, and our communities think we should be.

A successful life cannot be lived on the surface of the material life. Life's success is about *how* you live your life, no matter what your role in life is. Success in life comes from within and has nothing to do with material values. Success is not about triumphs, victories, conquests, wealth, or fame.

Living a happy, content, satisfied, and fulfilled life is a choice only you can make for yourself. Life's success is inner peace, contentment, and satisfaction as a result of striving to live the values of the Truth and living your life authentically.

2

Why Are We Here?

We enter this life with our souls and our karma, and we leave with these and nothing more. Each of us enters this life as a unique and special individual with a role to fulfill for the growth of our souls. When we leave this earth, all the worldly material stuff stays behind, and our human qualities die with our physical bodies. Human life is an illusion, but the life of our soul is not.

Why are we here? Man has been an explorer of the world and a student of life since the beginning of time. Many spend time trying to solve this question and unlock the mysteries of life, hoping to find the answers. We search outside of ourselves for the answers, hoping to find some kind of physical proof, without realizing the answers are not physical. The answers we are searching for can only be found in the Truth, and the knowledge of the Truth is within our souls. The exploration of the soul is the key to discovering the meaning of life and why we are here.

The exploration of the soul cannot be accomplished by science or searching the material world for answers. The exploration of the soul requires going within, becoming conscious and connecting with the soul. The result is the awareness and realization of the Truth, and of our oneness with God (the source of our existence). This is the discovery and satisfaction of the need to understand the mysteries of life, to realize what really matters, and to achieve true inner peace, contentment, and satisfaction.

We are so busy living unconsciously that we have become blind to what really matters. We are only aware of what matters when our lives are not working or when a crisis affects our lives. When our lives are out of balance is when we learn life's greatest lessons. The turbulent nature of the world today and our complicated, fast-paced lives are causing us to ask the questions, "Why am I here?" and "What is life really about?"

To realize why we are here is to realize what truly matters in life by becoming conscious of the Truth. Jesus Christ and the other ascending masters spent time on earth to teach us why we are here. Man's ego, realizing the power of their message, has taken the message and defined it to fit man's needs. This has created the distortions, confusion, and misunderstandings of why we are here.

We are here to learn the values of the Truth no matter what human activities we are performing. This is to learn the lessons that we agreed to learn for this lifetime, to fulfill our purpose, and to live for the betterment of all mankind, creation, and ourselves. Life's lessons are learned from our experiences. We are here to learn not only from our own experiences, but also from the experiences we share with each other. All of life's lessons lead to learning the values of the Truth, and the values of the Truth are the *cause* of life's lessons. When you live your life based on the values of the Truth, you will become aware of the knowledge of the Truth and the Truth of Human Life. You will discover who you are, why you are here, and what life is about.

Becoming conscious is going within and connecting with your soul. This is the discovery of who you are and what really matters. The awareness of the Truth is within each of our beings, but it is breaking free from the unconscious stigmas and traditions that is the challenge. What is important in life is living the awareness of the knowledge within our souls. This is striving to learn and live the values of the Truth as a result of learning life's lesson.

The purpose of human life is for the growth and development of our souls as we learn life's lessons on the path to enlightenment. Each of us has a different path to follow, but the lessons we learn are all the same. We are guided on our path by living consciously from the knowledge within our souls, and by the divine guidance we receive from God and the Universe. Living consciously is being an active participant or co-creator in your life's journey. Living unconsciously is like existing in the shadow of your life by simply going through the motions.

I do not have all the answers, but I do know the answers can be found in God's message of the Truth and by striving to learn and live the values of the Truth. It is by becoming conscious and connected with your soul that you will discover the answers to the meaning of your life. I cannot tell you how or when it will happen for you, but I do know if you have the sincere desire, take the time to take stock of your life, and become conscious, you will find the answers you need to have a successful journey in life.

The message of this text may sound simplistic, idealistic, or even complicated and unrealistic, but it is the Truth. The knowledge to realize why we are here and the knowledge to complete the journey of this lifetime is within each of our souls. This may not be what you were expecting to hear, but as you read, and if you pause and quiet your mind, you will find the Truth within your soul.

We are living in a great time of change, and the next frontier is not further exploration of the wonders of earth and space. The next frontier is the exploration of our souls and the search for consciousness. It is up to us to focus on why we are here, realize what truly matters, and create an environment that supports a conscious lifestyle.

Part 1

3

Clarifications

Out of respect for the many different faiths, religions, and spiritual beliefs, the following is a clarification for this text.

The Higher Power, One Divine Source, aka "God"

God is the name I am using to describe the one divine source of all creation throughout this text. It does not matter what name you use to refer to the one divine source, you can choose any name you like. Just understand that I am acknowledging the one divine source as "God." I will also be referring to God as 'he,' since this is how God has been traditionally referred to.

When God is mentioned, most often people think of religion. The God I am referring to in this text is our creator, and is the God of all creation and all religious faiths. God is the reason our souls exist, and the reason for our existence on this planet. There is one God. It does not matter whether you are Christian, Hindu, Islamic, Jewish, Buddhist, New Age, Native American, no faith, etc. What name you use to refer to the one divine source is up to you. Be it God, Yahweh, Allah, Jehovah, or any name you choose, do not get hung up on the name anyone uses to refer to the one divine source. It is the message of the one divine source and not the name that is important.

God is the one source, creator and master of all that is, and all that we have no knowledge of. God is the source of all the ascending masters which include Jesus Christ, Moses, Buddha, Abraham, Mohammad, etc. The ascending masters were sent by God to deliver to us his message of the Truth. If your affiliation is to one of the ascending masters, feel free to use his name in place of God as it applies to your beliefs.

In this text when I am referring to the "Universe," I am referring to the ascending masters, angels, and spirit guides collectively as a group, all of which are highly advanced and not equivalent with our souls. They are available to us for support, guidance, and for any reason that we might have during our earthly journey toward enlightenment. When you communicate with the Universe, you are communicating with God.

Eternal Life, the Afterlife

Our souls are eternal and immortal. When the body dies our souls return home to that part of creation we refer to as the afterlife, home, heaven, or whatever you would prefer to call it depending on your beliefs. When the soul leaves this earth, the only thing it takes is its karma.

I believe heaven has many different levels that are aligned with the various levels of our soul's development, where we continue to learn and grow, where positive help and assistance is provided, and from which we reincarnate back to earth or to another plane for further growth and development. The growth of the soul is a continuous process in which there can be advancement as well as regression during the process.

The life and growth of the soul is a continuous process with the goal of enlightenment. It is not about going to heaven or hell as a final destination when a soul passes on from this earth. First of all there is no a place called hell where any of us are left to suffer for all of eternity. Hell is a concept that was created by early religious leaders. The threat of hell was used for the purpose of power, control, intimidation, and judgment. When the soul leaves this earth, it continues on its journey toward enlightenment.

Reincarnation is one of the ways the soul advances as it moves along on its journey toward enlightenment. This is a process in which our souls experience the different levels of consciousness. Our souls continue to learn and develop whether it's on this earth, on another plane, or in heaven.

I believe we reincarnate many times on our journey to enlightenment as part of the learning process. How the process works is one of the mysteries. What we have to rely on are the accounts from those that have had near death experiences and what we know to be true from within our souls. There have been many accounts of near death experiences, and all near death experiences share a commonality in the experience and in the message. Books by Betty Eadie, *Embraced by Light*, and Dannion Brinkley, *Saved by the Light,* are two wonderful sources.

Mankind

When I am referring to mankind, man, human beings, or the population, I am referring to every man, woman, and child on the planet. This includes every race, color, and nationality. God makes no distinction between us. It is only man that makes the distinction. We are collectively the human race, equal in soul and spirit, and this is our common bond. We are all one regardless of faith, sex, race, color, or nationality.

Levels of Consciousness and Different Life Paths

When I am referring to the level of consciousness, I am referring to the level at which an individual is connected to their soul and their oneness with God. This can even be thought of as the level of lightness or darkness, or the level of positive energy and negative energy one has within their being. The levels vary from one person to another due to the balance of positive and negative energy. The soul is the source of our consciousness, and the ego is the source of our unconsciousness. Our level of consciousness is a balance of the two. All of us are at various levels of consciousness. This is necessary to create a balance in the world and is necessary for us to be able to learn from each other.

The path each of us is on in life varies from one person to another. Each path has a purpose with lessons to be learned. The different levels of consciousness and the paths we are on can be related to the different grades in school. A first grader cannot be compared to a sixth grader or a freshman in high school. It is easy for us to see that a first grader is not equivalent to the sixth grader or the freshman. We do not consider them to be the same, and we accept them as they are at their different levels and paths without question. The same holds true for an honor student in the sixth grade as compared to a "C" student in the sixth grade, however we do not see this the same way. Man's ego considers the "C" student to be inferior to the honor student. In reality, they are just at different levels and on different paths, with one not being any more important or better than the other. Each has a role to fulfill for the purpose of the growth of our individual souls, and our differences are necessary for the purpose of the whole.

It is perfectly fine if any of your views differ. What is important is the universal message of this text, which is to become conscious, connected with your soul and your oneness with God, and to live the values of the Truth by living your best life authentically.

4

Soul-Spirit, Ego-Mind

The human being is the union of two parts, the physical and nonphysical. The nonphysical is the soul and the spirit. The physical parts are the ego-mind, subconscious mind, and body. One of life's challenges is to find balance and harmony in order to align the nonphysical and the physical parts of our lives.

The Soul-Spirit

The soul and the spirit are united as one, and the two are interchangeable when referred to in this text. The soul-spirit is the immortal and eternal part of our being.

The soul and spirit are often referred to as our inner self, higher self, and authentic self. Our soul is who we really are. The soul is not attached to the material world or its possessions. The existence of the soul in human form is to experience human life for the purpose of learning life's lessons, fulfilling life's purpose, and realizing our oneness with God on the journey toward enlightenment as part of the soul's growth and development. God is the light of our souls, and the soul is the essence and energy of our human form. God's light is symbolic of his image, and his complete unconditional love and positive energy.

The soul knows the Truth and holds all the answers needed for you to learn life's lessons, fulfill your life's purpose, and live an authentic life. The soul is the navigator of your life, and you are directed by your soul through its intuition and divine guidance. Becoming conscious is to empower your soul and invite divine guidance into your life. When you empower the soul, you become confident and in charge of your life. This will give you the faith and the trust needed to follow your life's path and to live the values of the Truth. The soul is clear in its guidance with definite yeses and noes, not maybes. The soul does not see life's experiences as problems that are either positive or negative, but as lessons to be learned. The soul is not concerned with the topic of a particular experience, but is interested in the cause of the experience necessary to learn life's lessons as related to the values of the Truth.

The human life of the soul is about learning life's lessons. Our karma, intuition, thoughts, emotions, and feelings attract to us what we need to learn during this lifetime. Life is about learning the cause of our experiences as related to learning the values of the Truth. We do not attract to our lives that which we do not need to deal with in some way. When we do not deal with the causes of the experiences in our lives, the same issues will keep recurring.

The soul has no need for power or control, and not needing power makes the soul all-powerful. The soul does not value money, possessions, or status, since these are worldly illusions of values that have no real meaning. The soul does not rely on the approval of others, and is not affected by external influences. Only the soul knows what is true from what is false. The subconscious mind will believe either, while the ego-mind is not able to tell the difference.

The soul characteristics are the values of the Truth. The soul seeks light and positive energy. Light and all that is positive feeds the soul. The goal of the soul is to become one with

God, and this is why all paths lead to enlightenment. Being connected to your soul is being connected to God.

The soul is the immortal, eternal, and the highest part of our being. The soul never dies, it merely continues on the path toward enlightenment. How this works is not within the comprehension of our human minds, and is not important or relevant to having a successful journey on this planet. The focus and purpose of our lives is for the growth and development of our souls for this lifetime, not about dwelling on the mysteries of life. Becoming conscious and connected to our souls leads us to the awareness of the Truth, and gives each of us all the answers we need to focus on the lessons of this lifetime.

Many refer to the soul figuratively as their heart. This is not the physical heart, but the nonphysical, feeling heart. When you feel from the heart, you are in touch with your soul. When you follow your heart, you are following the intuition of your soul and divine guidance. However, it is important to note that the feelings of the ego-mind can feel like the feelings of your heart due to the controlling influence of the ego-mind.

To get in touch with your soul, think of it as a large single-story house, circular in shape with no windows, only solid doors that go all the way around the exterior. This house has no rooms except one room in the center with a single door, and this room contains the light of God. God's door is always open unless you close it, but his light never fails to shine. God's light (unconditional love) shines continuously and equally in each of us whether his door is opened or closed.

To allow light into your life, you must open the doors to your soul. Learning life's lessons and striving to live the values of the Truth will open the doors to your soul. Opening the doors to your soul will connect you with the light of God's love.

The Truth is light and positive energy with the ability to open wide all the doors of your soul. Negative energy closes doors, creates darkness, and is darkness. Negative energy is the result of fears, nontruths, neediness, greed, dishonesty, and lack of integrity. When the doors to your soul are closed, it is easy to get lost in the darkness, and it becomes very difficult to find your way through life. When you are able to open doors to your soul even slightly by attempting to sincerely live the values of the Truth, you will have the light necessary to see your way, and as you open more doors your path will become clearer.

It is important to understand the doors to your soul open and close based on your karma, the thoughts you have and the choices you make in life. This affects the amount of light available for you to see with. The more fears, turmoil, and drama you invite into your life, the less light there is, and the darker the darkness becomes and the more lost in life you become.

Inner peace is the feeling of contentment and satisfaction in life that comes from within your soul, and this is the realization of love. The material sources of satisfaction in life are an illusion, and create a constant cycle of pleasure and pain. Only that which comes from within your soul is satisfying, consistent, and everlasting. When you have inner peace from within your being, your worldly needs will change, and you will see your life as a journey of learning and growth. As you advance spiritually, you will increase the intensity of the light (love and positive energy) as you open more doors to your soul, and as you become one with the light of God.

The Ego-Mind

The ego is the human side of our being, and is necessary for us to learn life's lessons. The ego creates the barrier to becoming conscious and connecting with our souls. The ego-mind sees God as an external source and power, not the internal light of our souls. Nothing about connecting with your soul makes sense to the ego-mind. The ego-mind is the source of our negative energy and the origin of our fears.

The ego-mind is conscious only of itself, and can only identify with the human form. Its values are based on the material aspects of human life. Its characteristics are vanity, pride, self-indulgence, righteousness, etc. The ego-mind seeks power, control, and the desire to win and be right, but the ego-mind lacks confidence and is really insecure and powerless. The desires of the ego appeal to the masses, and the superficial, materialistic life feeds the ego. The comfort zone of the ego is living an unconscious life.

The ego-mind is not capable of knowing or understanding the Truth, and it does not know the difference between what is true, false, right, or wrong. The ego-mind can only identify with the limits of our physical being and creates a false illusion that it is the reason for our existence. The life of the ego is not eternal and the ego dies when the body dies.

The value and needs of the ego-mind are based on material values, the approval of others, and influence of external sources. The ego thrives on the material joys of human life that are meaningless to the soul. The ego-mind is never satisfied, once it gets what it wants, there is always something else, newer, different, bigger, better.

The ego-mind loves drama, thrives on temptation, conflict, intrigue, and the sensationalism of drama, crime, violence, and tragedy as well as gossip, rumors, and ridicule. All of this feeds the ego, creating life's problems, conflicts, stresses, and frustrations, while living in the past or future rather than in the present moment. Many become addicted or lost in this lifestyle, creating negative energy, and closing doors to their souls.

The ego-mind protects itself by creating problems and melodramas, so it can become lost in the resulting self-pity by blaming others and becoming a victim. The ego-mind is not responsible for itself and feels that others cause its problems and experiences that are unpleasant, but it will take credit for any positive experiences that occur. The ego-mind is judgmental and narrow-minded in its thinking, and it feels everyone thinks the same way it does or at least they should. The ego-mind is capable of rationalizing any point that works to its advantage, and it will distort any truth to justify its existence. But, it is justice it receives without being aware of it, due to the Law of Karma.

The ego-mind is very childlike and does not think independently. It is easily manipulated, impressionable, and impulsive. In comparison to the soul-spirit, the ego-mind is like a flock of ducks. One starts to quack, they all start quacking; one is startled and flies off, then they all fly off impulsively, in a frenzy, without realizing the cause. The soul-spirit is an individual that is like an eagle soaring boldly on its own path. The eagle observes, makes decisions considering the cause and effect, and does not act on impulse or the influences of others.

The ego-mind is the source of our doubts and is attracted to temptation due to its nature. With all this said, it is important to realize that the ego-mind is not the enemy and should not be viewed as such. The ego is what makes us human and is necessary for us to learn life's lessons.

Superior Ego

A superior ego can also exist. This occurs when someone deludes themselves into thinking they are a selected person who knows God above all others, has special power, is in total control, and has all the answers. This develops when someone is no longer humble and they feel that they are the source of their own divine guidance.

Superior egos are often the leaders of large productions whose interest is actually about financial gain, power, control, and fame. Superior egos can also be found leading small isolated groups and cults. One example of a superior ego is Jim Jones. He was able to convince people to follow him and even to take their own lives.

A superior ego will not always appear as a leader. It can be anyone who thinks they are more connected and superior to others. Having a superior ego can also lead to taking illogical risks, due to the feeling of being special and above the limits of human form, or when you are no longer humble. You cannot jump off a cliff or live life recklessly and expect God and the angels to catch you.

The Subconscious Mind

The subconscious mind holds your thoughts, emotions, and feelings, whether they are from your ego, your soul, or a result of your karma. Your subconscious mind works automatically, just as your heart beats automatically. You cannot tell your heart to stop beating and you cannot stop your subconscious thoughts from being revealed in your life, but you can change them.

The subconscious mind is like a warehouse that accepts at face value every thought, intention, emotion, feeling, fear, joy, etc., that you have. Within your subconscious mind is what you really think, how you really feel, and what you truly believe at any given time in your life. This also includes all the negative and positive programming as a result of your life's experiences.

The good news is the subconscious mind is trainable and will follow any direction without question or doubt. You can change your thoughts and your energy. The bad news is the subconscious mind can be programmed by propaganda, cultural influences, or any other external influences. It literally believes what you program it to believe, with no attachments. To change a thought you have to do more than just think about it. Merely thinking a thought is not enough. The change will not occur and the new thought will not become ingrained in your subconscious until you believe it, feel it, and live it. To learn life's lessons and live the values of the Truth, you will need to address and remove the negative programming and any nontruths within your subconscious mind. If you do not remove the negative programming and replace it with positive, it will continue to surface.

You draw to your life that which is in your subconscious. Like attracts like. You automatically feel comfortable with those who are like you subconsciously. You may even notice a trait you consider to be a fault in others, but fail to see it in yourself. You may think others create some of your problems or you attract bad luck, but you only attract to you that which you are as a result of your subconscious thoughts and your karma. No matter how good of an actor you are, your subconscious thoughts will come through. This will occur no matter how much you think you are in control. So, no matter what you say or what image you think you are projecting, what is in your subconscious will be reflected. Your ego-mind may think it is showing the world that you are confident, happy, and success-ful on the outside, while on the inside you are insecure and unhappy. You will draw to yourself others who are insecure and unhappy, whether you realize it or not. The reverse is also true.

Deep down each of us know when our lives are not work-ing. We self-sabotage our lives when we are not consciously aware of our subconscious. The ego allows us to fool ourselves into thinking we are what we see on the surface. It is up to each of us to get in touch with our thoughts, emotions, and feelings and to discover why we feel the way we do. This is necessary to change our thoughts and to align them with the values of the Truth.

When you live the values of the Truth, you will be able to program your subconscious with the positive knowledge of your soul. We are creatures of habit and change is not easy. It takes courage, desire, and determination to connect with your soul and change your thoughts, your energy, and your life.

The Body

The physical body is not who we are. We are nonphysical energy beings (souls), living in a physical body, having a human experience. The body is the earthly home for the soul.

This is why the body should be thought of as a temple and cared for as such. When the body is cared for with honor and respect, there will be honor and respect for the soul.

The care of your physical body not only includes nutrition and exercise, but becoming aware of your nonphysical self. Becoming conscious, connected to your soul, and living your life to feed your soul is just as important as feeding and proper care of your physical body.

Balancing the Physical and the Nonphysical

We live our lives in the illusion of our physical form, and the reality of who we are can only be lived from within our souls. The soul is our vision to realize what life is about. The ego represents the false self and is the blindness that blocks the soul's vision. The ego sees only the illusions of life as applied to the material world. The ego is the obstacle that keeps us from living from within our souls and holds us back from discovering the Truth and our purpose in life.

A balanced life lived between the physical and the nonphysical is very difficult to achieve, and knowing the difference between the two is a challenge. Creating a balanced life requires you to love and accept all the physical and nonphysical aspects of your being, all your positive and negative qualities, and to realize your ego is going to be involved in your life to some degree, no matter how conscious you may become. It is important to love and accept all of you, because you cannot change or enhance that which you do not acknowledge and accept.

A balance is created by becoming conscious and connected to your soul, and striving to live life according to the values of the Truth. It is the ego-mind that will continue to create the doubts and imbalances in your life, and this is why striving to live consciously is a continuous process.

God wants us to live happy, full, and abundant lives. God

wants us to have all the wonderful things in life that make us comfortable. It is when the material comforts become who we are and the focus of our lives that we lose our way. Life is to be lived from the inside out (from within your soul), not on the surface (the ego-dominated material life). A life lived on the surface ignores the presence of the soul.

Life is a continuous balancing act between the soul-spirit and the ego-mind. The ego-mind is absorbed with itself and seeks power, control, being right, and striving to win. The ego-mind is capable of influencing your thoughts and intentions, even when you are devoted to living the Truth. The subconscious will believe what you program it to believe whether the information comes from your ego, an exterior source, or from the knowledge within your soul.

When you empower the soul-spirit by becoming conscious, the ego-mind will be silenced and retreat easily, but only temporarily. The ego is like a child that is attached to the superficial, material world, always waiting for a weak moment to pull you back into your old familiar ways. When you give an inch, the ego-mind takes a mile. It is important to maintain structure and discipline to keep the ego in line, just as you would a child. The ego-mind has no real power over the soul-spirit. The only power the ego-mind has is that which you allow it to have.

The soul has all the knowledge and power you need to live an authentic life. It is just waiting for you to make the connection and become conscious. It is necessary to understand the role of the ego-mind so you can silence it. The ego-mind is merely a challenge and a necessary part of the learning process. Finding a balance in life is not easy unless you realize the ego–mind likes to create a constant struggle, a tug-of-war, so to speak, with the soul, and can become a real barrier if you allow it. Even as you become aware and conscious, you may still feel as if you are failing miserably. Just know if you are struggling with your ego and striving to live the values of the

Truth, you are accomplishing more than you are giving yourself credit for.

When you try to balance your life, consider the following example. Your physical being is a boat floating down the river of life. The boat is your body. This is the only boat you are going to have for this lifetime, so you are going to have to care for it and maintain it in order for it to last. The ego-mind is the crew and the soul-spirit is the captain. The soul/captain has the knowledge (the compass) and is able to chart the course necessary for you to achieve your life's journey. This is the ultimate scenario.

The more likely scenario goes something like this. The soul/captain is relaxing in the cabin down below while the ego/crew is at the controls, in charge of the boat, and floating along without a compass. The soul/captain lets the ego-crew know in a whisper it has the knowledge to set the course. Naturally, due to the pride of the ego/crew, the soul/captain is ignored. The soul/captain will wait patiently to be acknowledged, since it knows life's lessons are learned by experience.

The ego/crew insists on doing everything itself and appears confident. The ego/crew desires to be right and absolutely does not want to lose the power and control it feels. Frustration and stress occurs when the ego/crew keeps making mistakes and errors, not learning from its experiences. The ego/crew sets the course, but something usually happens and things do not always go as planned. The ego/crew really has no real control over where the boat is going, no idea of the destination, but keeps insisting that it does. The ego/crew feels the soul/captain is worthless, after all the soul/captain just sits down below whispering what the ego/crew needs to do to get on course. Besides, what could the soul/captain possible know that the ego/crew does not? The soul/captain will only help when acknowledged, and the ego/crew must step aside from the controls for this to happen.

The ego/crew feels that floating down the river of life is a constant struggle it must win to be successful. Winning what, the ego-mind it is not sure, but it knows when you win you will have it all and life will be good, if only for a short time. When the focus is on winning, conflict is always present. The ego/crew will only surrender to the soul/captain for help when it is frustrated, lost, and desperate from being off course.

When you allow the ego/crew to navigate your life, the journey will always be off course and unable to reach its final destination. The soul/captain has the compass and knows which direction to follow to have a successful journey in life. The soul/captain is also able to navigate the boat back on course, no matter what choices the ego/crew has made, or how far off course your life is. It is never too late to get back on course with your life. Unless the soul/captain is navigating the boat, the journey will remain off course. Keep in mind it only takes a small change in degrees of the compass to be miles off course on your life's journey.

You have to surrender and let go of your ego-mind in order to connect with your soul-spirit. Once you connect with your soul and allow your soul to start running your life, things will fall into place. This does not mean nirvana. You are still human and your life is about learning from all your experiences, both good and bad. It means you will begin seeing experiences and situations in a different light. You will realize problems only exist in your ego-mind, and good and bad experiences have positive value in the learning process.

Searching for the perfect balance is difficult, since change is always occurring. Part of balancing your life is learning to go with the flow, trusting in the intuition of your soul, and accepting and learning as you move forward. Living the Truth and becoming conscious will create balance and harmony in your life.

Part 2

5

The Truth

The Truth is God's message taught to us by Jesus Christ and the other ascending masters. *God's message of the Truth is love.* The realization of the Truth comes from within your soul, and you must *feel it to know it.*

The Truth and its meaning is pure, basic, simple, constant, consistent, timeless, and uncomplicated. The Truth has no secrets, causes no harm or punishment, creates positive energy, and is positive energy. The Truth contains no evil forces, negativity, or negative energy. The Truth is eternal and the same for all time, for all people. All spiritual experiences with God are the same.

God's message of the Truth is inherent within each of us and is innately imprinted upon our souls. We are naturally bound to the Truth from within the inner consciousness of our souls. It is up to each of us individually to become aware of it, acknowledge it, feel it, know it, and then live it.

The Truth and its meaning is nonnegotiable. The Truth is universal, unites all faiths, and remains the same, regardless of one's religious faith, philosophy, or spiritual orientation. The Truth is at the foundation of all faiths and is taught by all faiths in some manner, but applying it to everyday life and living it is not. When you live the Truth and are devoted to the Truth, the knowingness will automatically reveal itself to you, and the many doors to your soul will begin to open. Living the Truth is a continuous learning process that never stops.

The way to discover the Truth is to become conscious of the knowledge within your soul. As you discover the Truth, you will become empowered. This will cause your entire life to change. This change may occur in an instant, but usually occurs gradually over time with advancing moments of clarity. It is not important how it happens or when it happens, just that you *realize it* when it does. Desire, courage, commitment, determination, and discipline are required for those seeking the Truth.

It is possible for someone to live the values of the Truth and have no knowledge of God or believe in him. Many religious faiths would disagree with this concept, but it is the distortions of the Truth and fears of man's ego that has created the misconceptions and judgments of others, not God's message. God's love, light, and positive energy is in all that he creates whether there is the awareness of his presence or not. Living a life based on the values of the Truth is living the Truth. This is true whether someone believes in God or not.

We are living in a great time of change and spiritual advancement. Life as we know it is changing due to the number of people seeking the awareness of the Truth and their oneness with God. This will gradually create an environment of positive energy that will offset a good deal of the negative energy that currently exists. This is a gradual process, but over time, as the level of integrity of mankind increases, our world will change. We are already beginning to see some of the changes, and we will continue to see many more. We will begin to see governments and business practices changing. Greed, intolerance, and prejudice will not be looked upon favorably and will begin to diminish. Religious faith will begin shifting back to the foundation of the teachings of the Truth. As the level of spiritual consciousness of mankind increases, the tolerance of nontruths and any practices that lack integrity will be tolerated less and less. A new peaceful world is on the horizon.

The Truth Is:

1. There Is One Divine Source

2. God's Love Is Unconditional for All Mankind

3. We Are All Created Equal, We Are All One, All Our Souls Are Interconnected

4. The Soul Is Eternal

5. The Truth Is Inherent Within Each of Us

6. The Golden Rule

7. The Law of Karma

8. The Values of the Truth

9. Faith

There Is One Divine Source

There is one God that is the master and creator of all that is, and all that God has created is good. There is one source for all creation and this includes the ascending masters, angels, spirit guides, and all mankind.

God created us in his image and he resides within the souls of each of us. His image is within our souls and is not about our physical appearance. God's image is his light, love, and positive energy. God is everywhere at all times, and all mankind has a direct connection to God at all times. We are never abandoned by or separated from God. To know God is to feel his love from within. God's presence is realized by becoming conscious and connected with our souls. The divinity of God is in all of us, and realizing the Truth brings this into being.

The belief in God is a belief that must be realized and

based on faith. The mysteries and unknowns of God and life are not for us to figure out. As humans we do not have the capacity to understand all the details, and God is beyond our comprehension as related to human form. We have been given what we need to know and we are shown only that which we are able to understand.

God's Love Is Unconditional for All Mankind

The essence of God is love. God's love is unconditional with complete compassion and forgiveness for all mankind. God's love is complete, pure, positive energy and has absolutely no qualities of negative energy. As humans we find this hard to understand, since we deal with both positive and negative energy as part of our learning process.

God's love is pure, rich, radiant, solid, secure, and complete. The energy of God's love is the light within your soul. Experiencing God's love is to feel true joy and contentment from within. To know and feel God's love is the finest, most complete, whole feeling imaginable. God's love feels unlike any other feeling of love you have experienced. It is a feeling that is deeper, richer, more whole and complete than can be described in words. The spiritual experience of God's love will change the meaning of your life.

Unconditional love describes *how* we are loved, and each of us is loved at all times, no matter what. God's love has no requirements. The light of God's love shines within the soul of each and every human being. No one, absolutely no one, is without or beyond God's love. This is true for every man, woman, and child whether they believe in him or not. The evidence of God's love is in the reality of our creation, in the reality of what matters in life, and in his message of the Truth that is demonstrated to us as we learn life's lessons.

Man's ego has been making value judgments about God's love for thousand of years. The ascending masters taught us that God's love is unconditional and that we do not have the ability to make judgments on his behalf, yet we continue to do so. It is believed by many that we anger God with our "sins." God has been portrayed as totalitarian, authoritarian, and a source of punishment. God's love is not emotional and it is not about punishment, judgment, retaliation, or intimidation, as many would like to believe. These are all nontruths and require negative energy to exist. The positive energy of God's love is all loving and all giving. God does not sit on a throne looking down upon us in judgment. What he does is shine the light of his love into each one of us, and becoming conscious is to realize this.

Many find it hard to understand God's unconditional love, since human life is difficult. We rationalize that if God loved us so much then how could he let bad things happen. It is man's ego that has rationalized that God or some other force is the cause of bad things happening. The opposing forces we deal with come from our own egos and karma. No other sources exist. Human life is about learning life's lessons for the growth of the soul, and without the good and bad experiences, we would not be able to learn.

God's love is within each and every one of us, and it is up to each of us to become aware of it. When you are conscious and connected to your soul, you are connected to your oneness with God and his love. Even the slightest connection is sufficient to know and feel the love, and to be able to grow from within your soul. Know that above all else, God loves you absolutely, unconditionally, at all times, no matter what.

We Are All Created Equal, We Are All One, All Our Souls Are Interconnected

We are souls before we are anything else, and realizing this is to know that we are all one. We are energy beings and it is our energy that connects us to one another. It is our energy that draws to us the relationships we have in life, and it is our energy that makes us part of the whole of mankind. Our souls are all interconnected. We are one big family.

Everyone is created equal. No one is any better or worse, higher or lower, or more superior or inferior than anyone else. God and the Universe see no differences in race, color, ethnic background, nationality, male, female, rich, poor, smart, or challenged. We are all seen as equal no matter what religion, philosophy, or faith, be it eastern, western, agnostic, atheist, or pagan. The only difference is we are all on different paths and at different levels of consciousness in this journey of life. Each of us is part of the whole; each of us has our own role to play.

The concept of we are all created equal is hard to grasp at first, but it is the Truth. Here is an example of how we are equal at the human level, and that basic life is and has been the same for all time. Motherhood is universal and the bond between a mother and child is the same no matter what race, color, nationality, culture, or faith. The needs of every baby and small child are the same. When a baby or small child is not nurtured and shown love, they will fail to develop and thrive, and in some cases even die. All of us require the same necessities to exist. Our hearts beat the same, and we laugh, cry, and feel pain the same. A smile is a smile, no matter whose face it is on. Our only differences lie in the appearance of our physical exteriors, our various levels of consciousness, and the various paths each of us is on.

We are all God's children, and we are all brothers and sisters sharing this planet. We are different externally and culturally for a reason. If we were meant to be the same, we would have been created that way. The relationships we have with each other are for the purpose of teaching us a great deal about ourselves. We need to respect, accept, and embrace our differences. Becoming conscious allows us to realize how similar we are, and this enables us to learn love, integrity, humility, peace, compassion, and forgiveness, which are life's greatest lessons.

Our lives are all interrelated as if we are one big symphony. Events are not random. They fall into place due to our energy and the free will choices we make. Our interaction and reaction affect not only us but others, due to the energy each of us generates. The effect of our energy directly and indirectly affects the energy balance of everyone we are involved with and that of nature and the environment.

We are all one. All our souls are created by God. The light of God shines equally in the soul of every human being on this earth, regardless of any differences we might think exist. Turmoil and conflict will continue until we put aside our differences, created by our egos, and realize we are all one. Oneness is a reality that comes from within our souls.

The Soul Is Eternal

The soul-spirit of our being is eternal and it has no beginning or end. Only physical life begins and ends. The reality of death of the physical body is a wake-up call that causes us to value life. It is in valuing life that we realize love is all that matters. This Truth is important because it reminds us to keep in perspective why we are here, to realize there is a reason for our earthly existence, and to realize how much of our lives is spent on unimportant, superficial, material matters.

The life of the soul continues after the death of the body. Jesus Christ through his teachings taught us about eternal life, enlightenment, and the salvation of our souls. With his resurrection, Jesus Christ demonstrated to us, and gave us the awareness, that life is eternal and that enlightenment and salvation are the result of faith. Due to the tragic manner of his death and the turbulent nature of the times, the meaning of eternal life, enlightenment, and salvation have been misunderstood.

Eternal life of our souls is not something we earn, it occurs naturally and is not the result of the death of Jesus.

Enlightenment occurs in varying degrees and does not have a pass or fail requirement. Enlightenment is becoming one with God, occurring due to the growth of our souls as a result of becoming conscious, learning life's lessons, and striving to live the values of the Truth. Enlightenment is what our souls hunger for, and it is the meaning of life that we seek. Enlightenment is our salvation.

The Truth Is Inherent Within Each of Us

Each of us is born with the inner knowing of the Truth within our souls. Each of us literally means every man, woman, and child that has ever existed and exists today. Absolutely no one is left out. Everyone has the same amount. No one has any more or any less. Some may appear to have more than others due the various levels of consciousness, but it is important to understand that there is not a ranking of superiority or inferiority for our souls. Only the ego-mind believes we are valued at different levels. Status in life according to worldly values has no bearing on God's view of us.

The knowledge of the Truth is available to all of us equally. It is up to us individually to become aware of the knowledge within our souls by becoming conscious. Everything we need to become conscious is available to each of us from within; it is the matter of whether we desire to connect with it or not. We possess the knowledge of the Truth within, and connecting with our souls is the only way to *feel it* and *know it*. However, until it is acknowledged and realized, we are blind to its presence.

Each of us is born with a spiritual hunger and a natural desire to connect with our souls and to our oneness with God. Once the awareness of the knowledge of the Truth within your soul is tapped, you will be drawn to it like a magnet. Once you become aware of the Truth, you will not be able to hide from it or deny its presence, but you can choose to ignore it. If you choose to ignore what you feel, you will feel as if your life is missing something and your life will be filled with discontentment and dissatisfaction. All mankind has the ability to become aware of the Truth from within their souls.

The Golden Rule

The Golden Rule is one of the greatest gifts ever taught to mankind by the ascending masters. The Golden Rule teaches the values of the Truth, with love being the result of practicing peace, integrity, humility, compassion, forgiveness, tolerance, and nonjudgment. These basic principles resonate in the teachings of the ascending masters and are at the foundation of all religious faiths.

The Golden Rule is stated as, "Love your neighbor as yourself." "Do unto others as you would have them do unto you." "Do unto yourself, as you would have others do unto you." "Honor others as you honor yourself." "Treat yourself and others as you would like to be treated." The Golden Rule teaches us to not only love others we get along with, but our enemies as well.

The Golden Rule literally means to live with integrity and treat others with love, dignity, respect, honesty, compassion, and forgiveness. This is to respect and care for others even if you do not agree with their choices in life or their beliefs. When you are true to yourself and treat yourself with love, compassion, forgiveness, integrity, honor, and respect, you will treat others this way by practicing goodwill toward all and by being ethical, honest, and fair in all your dealings.

The Golden Rule instructs us to live for the betterment of all mankind, including ourselves. To not practice the Golden Rule is to *knowingly* cause harm to yourself, others, or any part of creation. This includes any opportunistic intentions involved in taking advantage of a situation for self-gratifying reasons and/or the exploitation of others.

The Truth is absolute; however, it is necessary to under-

stand that for human beings the Golden Rule appears to be sub-
jective. The subjectivity is of our ego-minds and not of our
souls. This occurs when we compare ourselves to others and
when we judge others. It is not for us to use the Golden Rule to
evaluate or to judge anyone. Everyone is capable of understanding and has the knowledge of the Golden Rule in its true
form within our souls; however, the misunderstanding occurs
since we are all at different levels of consciousness. The
Golden Rule is absolute as we see it for ourselves and we
expect it to be the same way for others. We tend to think others
see things the same way we do.

When you are true to yourself, the Golden Rule is not sub-
jective. When you are true to your level of consciousness, the
Golden Rule will be absolute for your actions and intentions. A
life based on nontruths and lacking in integrity will view the
Golden Rule differently than someone that lives with integrity
and is striving to live the values of the Truth. Realize it is the
interpretation of our egos that is flawed and not the Rule itself.

In our superficial society, the Golden Rule has become,
"Do unto others before they do unto you," "Do unto others
what benefits me," "The end justifies the means," and "Nice
guys finish last." As long as we are able to get ahead and win
or get the results we want, it does not matter how we get there
or who we run over in the process. This is demonstrated time
and again in our legal system, in the world of business, and in
our daily lives. In the world today, it has become acceptable,
and a common practice, to twist and distort any truth to achieve
the desired outcome. This has resulted in a loss of integrity and
reverence, and lack of respect for ourselves, others, and life in
general.

The Golden Rule teaches us to base our relationships with
ourselves and others on the values of the Truth. We need to
understand that each of us are at different points of reference,
at various levels of awareness and consciousness, and we will
have differing views. We need to understand that not everyone

will respond to us the way we expect them to. The key is to realize the various levels of consciousness of those around you and those you come in contact with, and accept them for who they are. This does not mean you will need to include them in your life, but if you do, you will not allow them to affect your life. Adopt the attitude, "Forgive them for they know not what they do."

The Law of Karma

The Law of Karma is also known as the law of cause and effect, or *"Life is fair."* This means you alone are responsible for your life, past, present, and future, and this includes all your thoughts, choices, intentions, and actions. You are responsible for all the events that happen in your life. Once you realize this, you will no longer blame anyone else or any exterior source for the events and happenings of your life, and you will be able to learn.

Karma is the result of the experiences of your soul. During any lifetime, the karma you bring with you will be the karma you agreed to work on for that lifetime. The karma brought to this lifetime is about drawing to you the events and situations necessary for you to learn the lessons you agreed to. How you learn is up to you. You have the free will to change your karma by becoming conscious and discovering the *cause* of your thoughts, emotions, and feelings. Being able to realize the *cause* is being able to change the *effect* and change your life.

The cause and effect is about the balance of your energy. It is how you live your life and the lessons you learn that changes the balance of your energy. The phrase, "You reap what you sew," does not mean you are being punished. Negative karma is not about punishment being inflicted upon you. The punishment you think you are receiving is actually the affect of your own karma being reflected back to you so you can learn.

Everything happens for a reason. You have the ability to

create negative karma with negative thoughts, choices, intentions, and actions, and when you knowingly and intentionally
cause harm to yourself, others, or any part of God's creation.
You have the ability to create positive karma by striving to live
the values of the Truth, and when you are living your best life
for the betterment of yourself and all mankind. When you are
conscious, you will become aware of when your thoughts,
choices, intentions, and actions create positive or negative
energy. Your karma is the energy of your being. The effect of
your karma is both positive and negative, and the balance of
your energy is the balance of your karma.

Life's lessons are learned from both positive and negative
experiences, but it is the negative experiences that have the
greatest impact on our lives. Depending on how you live your
life and your attitude, you can change your energy and what
you attract to your life. When you are living the effects of your
negative karma, you will draw negative events, situations, and
relationships toward you, and this will continue until you learn.
When you choose to learn, you change and enhance the energy
of your being. This will result in changing the balance of your
energy and the nature of the events you draw into your life. You
can also change the events you draw to your life by focusing on
living the values of the Truth.

How karma works can be seen in our relationships. Our
relationships with others are mirrors of ourselves. Like energy
attracts like energy. We reflect that which we are. What we
give, we get back. We do not realize this, but it is how others
respond to us that shows us how we really feel about ourselves,
and how we treat others is how we treat ourselves. It is our subconscious thoughts and feelings that direct our true intentions
and reflect who we truly are. It is our actions, the *how* we live
our lives, and *how* we treat others that speaks volumes. If you
are unhappy with life, you actually will not want others to be
happy and will not want to be around others who are. Misery
loves company, whether you realize it or not, and you will

attract others who are unhappy, regardless of how they appear on the surface. We realize we are affected by the views and behavior of others, but we often fail to realize how our own views and behavior actually affect us by drawing to us that which we project.

When you do not respect yourself, although you may not even realize it, you will disrespect others, and others will disrespect you because you actually make it easy for them to do so. When you truly love and respect yourself, you will love and respect others, and you will receive love and respect in return. This will happen automatically as a result of your energy. Being able to grasp and understand this concept will help you make changes in your life and in your relationships. Becoming aware of what you are reflecting will help you in learning life's lessons.

Karma is about learning life's lessons. Karma draws to us the situations that help us learn. Karma teaches us that it is the *causes* that generate the *effects* of our lives.

The Values of the Truth

God's message of the Truth is love, and the values of the Truth are love and its qualities of integrity, humility, peace, compassion, and forgiveness, providing goodwill and service to all mankind and creation. This is to have reverence, understanding, acceptance, tolerance, and respect for all that is.

Learning life's lessons is learning the values of the Truth, and all life's lessons lead to learning the values of the Truth. Learning love is at the core of all life's lesson. Love brings all the values of the Truth into alignment naturally and creates balance and harmony in life.

The values of the Truth are contagious. This is how you touch the lives of others resulting in a positive impact on them and the world. When you show kindness, understanding, and acceptance to anyone, you are validating their lives with love and compassion, and creating positive energy and a positive environment. In today's world, many are surprised by true acts of integrity, kindness, and caring. As more people begin to live the values of the Truth, acts of integrity, kindness, and caring will become the norm rather than the exception.

The values of the Truth are interconnected, if you work on learning the lessons of one, you will be working on all of them.

Love

The Truth is love. Love is the state of being of God and the Universe. Love is the state of being we are here to learn. Human life and all that seems so important on the surface is just an illusion; the reality of what matters is love.

Love is the awareness and knowledge of God's light and his positive energy within our souls. Love is the reality of our oneness with God, and knowing God's love is to no longer question the mysteries of life.

Love is the most positive and powerful energy that exists and is unconditional and consistent. It does not start or stop and it does not change. Love bears all and gives and receives freely. Love is the feeling of being whole and complete. Love has no conditions, creates no obligations, expectations, wants, or needs. Negative energy is not involved in any aspect of love. When there is love, there is no pain, hurt, or harm. The qualities of love are integrity, humility, peace, compassion, and forgiveness.

Love is the way to look at life's experiences and the way of relating to yourself and others with positive energy. Love is reflected in *how* you live your life and *how* you treat others. Love is the acceptance of life and respect for life. Love is the feeling of joy and inner peace you feel from within your being. Love feeds your soul, just as air, food, and water feed your body. Love is a state of being, and you are love when you live love.

Love for all mankind comes from the reality we are all one. It is knowing each of has the light of God within our soul. Love removes all judgments and prejudices, including cultural, ethnic, and racial biases. Love is reverence for all mankind and creation. Before you will be able to love anyone or all mankind, you will need to love yourself first. Self-love and honoring yourself is having self-esteem.

Every human being wants the same thing, to be loved. Love validates our lives and gives meaning to our lives. When love is not present in our lives, our lives become a shallow and meaningless existence. When you love yourself, you will not need love. When you feel love within your being, you will naturally love others by giving love, attracting love, and receiving love. You cannot give love or share love unless you are love. It is just not possible. You cannot give something you do not have. Being able to give and receive works the same way for tangible objects as well as the intangible. You cannot give your neighbor a cup of sugar, if you do not have sugar to give.

Love is what makes a difference in peoples lives. Love is respecting and accepting others as they are without wanting them to change. Love is treating others with respect, kindness, compassion, and forgiveness. This does not mean you will like or get along with everyone, but you will be able to treat others with kindness, dignity, and respect. Your actions will always speak louder than words. A genuine smile warms any heart. When you show others kindness and respect, you let them know they matter. This is a validation that shows and gives love to those in your personal life and those you randomly meet.

Love is a value of the Truth that is within your soul. Love is realized by becoming conscious and connected to your soul. If you are not connected to the love from within your soul, you will not be able to give love to yourself or others. To discover love and be love, you have to become aware of it, acknowledge it, feel it, know it, and then live it. When you are able to live love, love will be your state of being.

The ego-mind has a different understanding of what love is. The ego-mind believes love is conditional, based on need, and love from others will fill a void in your life. This is why so many relationships do not work. You cannot need love from others to create love for yourself.

Many times what we think is love is actually emotional involvement. Love is not the emotional state we know as romantic love, and it has nothing to do with physical attraction. Love is not something you earn. Love is not about being dependent, controlled, controlling, or possessive of someone or something. Love does not hurt, it is not painful, and it does not cause pain or harm. Love is felt from within your soul, and not from your ego-mind.

Love is life's most valuable lesson to be learned. When love is given freely and truly, you will love someone for who they are, and this will not change. To understand what unconditional means is to relate it to the love we have for babies and pets. We love them easily, unconditionally, with no expectations, and whether they give back or not, we accept their response. Love is not about what you want, what you need, or what you get from another person. Love is not something you work at. Love is a state of being from which you give. When you give love, love is returned.

The love we feel for others gives us insight into God's love. To relate to how God's love feels is to compare it to infatuated romantic love, except God's love is thousands of times stronger. When you are infatuated romantically, nothing else seems to matter. All problems and obstacles are handled easily as they occur, and everything in your life flows. God's love feels much the same way as infatuated romantic love, but without the highs, lows, or neediness. God's love is a consistent feeling of inner peace, joy, contentment, and satisfaction. It is feeling positive about life, no matter what is going on around you, and the ability to deal with life's obstacles, knowing all things will work out as they should.

Love is the answer to all questions and is the solution to all problems. Love has the ability to solve and heal all problems no matter if they are personal or related to the world. When there is love, there is always an answer. We know this to be true in our personal relationships, but it is also true for our relationships with all mankind. Love gives positive energy and impacts not only those around us, but the rest of the world. We just need to realize it and live it.

Nothing fills you up or makes you feel more whole than love. Love is your connection to God. Love is the ability to look at all creation and see the light of God in all people and in all things. Granted, this may be near to impossible in some cases, but the light is there. It is just covered up by a whole bunch of darkness (negative energy). Looking at all creation with love will change your life, the lives of others, and the world, by giving and reflecting positive energy.

Becoming conscious and connecting with your soul will access your awareness of love. You will know love when you *feel it* from within your soul. Love God above all else, and as you become one with God, you will become one with love. Strive to have love become a constant part of your being by living the Truth.

Peace

Peace is love. The qualities of peace are harmony, tranquility, and serenity. To be at peace, you must live peace. Living the values of the Truth creates peace.

Peace is what we say we want, but peace is not how we live our lives. When feelings of fear, anger, resentment, or the need to win are present, peace is not reflected and is not the result. You cannot control, dominate, or intimidate others to create peace. Conflict does not create peace. War has not, does not, and will not create peace. War is about dealing with effects and not causes. If war created peace, the world would be a very different place by now. War has the appearance of creating peace, since history is usually written by the victors. Great nations have risen and have fallen due to wars, and this will continue as long as conflict is seen as a way to create peace. Winning is not about peace and does not create peace. Winning is about domination, power, and control, all of which are negative energy. The winners do not see the losers as equals and losers feel defeated. The energy of the conflict remains.

You cannot be an advocate for peace by supporting anything that causes harm to another human being or any of God's creation. When you lack caring and consideration for others, and your focus is on conflict, you create negative energy. You cannot be about peace (positive energy) and be involved in conflict (negative energy) at the same time. Even demonstrations for peace are usually the result of anger and end in conflict. Peace cannot exist in the presence of negative energy.

Peace is created by cooperation and compromises, as a result of love and compassion for all parties. To have peace, all parties must be satisfied with the solution; there can be no winner or losers.

Gandhi is a wonderful example of being and living peace. His quest of India's independence from Britain was accomplished by nonviolence. His triumph was one of the complete will of love and peace, and the reflection of positive energy.

World peace will require the realization that we are all one, and that the light of God shines within each of us. When we are able to realize this, we will no longer destroy each other. This may or may not be possible, but we will not know if we do not try. As the song goes, "Let there be peace on earth and let it begin with me." One person can make a difference. Peace is a state of being. You have to live peace to be peace.

Integrity

Integrity is key to living the Truth. Integrity is living your best life, at your highest potential, for the greater good of God, yourself, all mankind, and creation. Integrity is being true to yourself, when you are true to yourself, you honor yourself, God, and all others. Integrity is the result of being connected to your soul, having self-esteem, and being responsible for your thoughts, actions, and intentions.

Integrity is honesty at all costs, and it accepts only that which you know to be true from within your soul. It is doing the right thing, no matter what the outcome. When choices and decisions are made based on integrity, the outcome will always be as it should be, no matter how it appears.

To live with integrity is to reflect love, humility, peace, compassion, and forgiveness.

Humility

Humility is the wisdom to discover the Truth. Humility is realizing you cannot become conscious without God's help. The qualities of humility are humbleness, empathy, reverence, respect, acceptance, honesty, fairness, and gratitude. Humility is the loss of or being without pride, arrogance, or self-importance. Humility silences the ego. The result of humility is reverence for all life.

Humility is gratitude for your existence. Realizing you have been given the gift of life, the gift of free will, everything happens for a reason, and you would not be who you are today without all the good and bad experiences of your life. Humility gives honor and value to the path you are on, and it is the gratitude that allows you to embrace life and focus on your life's journey.

Humility is realizing we are souls in human bodies, and we are all one. It is realizing all paths are important and it is accepting others for who they are. This is to realize no one is any better or more important than anyone else, each of us make mistakes and errors, and we do not have the ability to judge one another. Status in life according to cultural and worldly values has no bearing on how God and the Universe see us.

Humility is to be humble, no matter how much material and/or spiritual success you have. Humility will keep you on track or help you to get back on track if you lose your way. If you cross into the realm of feeling superior, you will no longer be grateful, your ego will control your life, and you will lose sight of who you are. Being humble keeps your feet on the ground and allows you to be your best and do your best. When you strive to live your best life, you inspire others to be their best. At the very least, you will leave an impression they can recall when they are ready.

Humility is the humbleness that awakens you to the reality of human life. This is the realization that the human existence is an illusion, that all the material stuff is just stuff. Humility takes you into your soul, and you realize what is on the inside is more important than what is on the outside.

Compassion

Compassion is treating yourself and others with love, dignity, and respect. Compassion is positive energy. It has the qualities of love, empathy, kindness, reverence, tolerance, service, goodwill, and the ability to see all mankind without judgment. Compassion is the ability to understand, accept, and forgive yourself and others. Compassion creates a positive attitude and a positive environment.

Compassion is not about feeling sorry for, having sympathy for, or pity for yourself or others. These are negative feelings that will only draw negative energy to any situation. Compassion gives love, encouragement, and support. This is assisting someone up, not holding them up by their bootstraps.

Compassion is to have empathy and understanding for the

difficulties of human life and to relinquish judgment. This is realizing we are human, all of us make mistakes, and all of our lives are very similar, yet respecting our differences. We can only imagine what another person's life is like. It is easy to have compassion for someone when you know them, but we tend to judge more harshly those we do not know. It is easy to have compassion when you can relate to a similar experience, but difficult when you have no concept. It is impossible to understand true hunger unless you have literally been starved. Imagining is just not the same. We tend to judge and fear anything that is not familiar or that we do not understand.

To have compassion is to not judge others and to become tolerant. This is knowing that given the same set of circumstances, you may not have done any better. This does not mean you condone or give approval to someone's actions. It is knowing you do not have the ability to judge anyone else's life. You cannot know someone's life unless you walk in their shoes, and it is impossible to walk in another man's shoes. Compassion is the realization of a bigger picture, and we are not capable of judging others by just the snapshot of the life we think we see.

Great wisdom is found in compassion; it is key to the Golden Rule, the realization we are all one. Compassion is caring about the well-being of all mankind. It is about helping others feel good about themselves, inspiring them to be their best, giving hope to those that need encouragement, and supporting them through the rough times as well as the good times.

Compassion is goodwill and the service of giving to all mankind and creation. Service and giving are not about sacrifice. Service, giving, and goodwill have many appearances, and they are not just about charity and helping those in need. Service is giving openly, freely, and genuinely from your heart as part of living life. When you strive to live your life with love, integrity, humility, peace, compassion, and forgiveness, you are serving all mankind and creation.

Service can be as simple as being courteous and showing

kindness to others. It can be as simple as a comment or as complex as living your life so that it affects and changes someone else's life in a positive way. Service is also being an inspiration to others by giving them the desire to move forward in their lives. As the saying goes, "Give a man a fish, feed him for a day; teach a man to fish, feed him for life." It is not just about feeding the hungry. It is helping through education and other appropriate ways to raise their standard of living so they are able to feed themselves. Service is about dealing with causes and changing the effects.

When you live with compassion, you will be creating positive energy for yourself and others whether you know it or not. You will be giving to the world and others just by creating positive energy. When you give freely, it comes back to you in more ways than you can imagine.

Forgiveness

Forgiveness is love and compassion for yourself and others. Forgiveness allows us to see the light of God within every human being. Forgiveness comes from within your soul. The ego is not capable of forgiving, does not want to forgive, and simply does not understand forgiveness.

Forgiveness is the ability to accept yourself and others. Humility and compassion are the ways to learn forgiveness, by silencing the ego and realizing that each of us is human. Ask yourself the question Jesus asked, "Who among you is able to cast the first stone (or any stone for that matter)?" Forgiveness is not about judgment and it does not seek justice or punishment.

The healing of forgiveness comes from within when you forgive yourself. Forgiveness is about making peace with yourself, learning to love yourself, and changing your energy from negative to positive. Changing your energy will affect others more than you know. When you forgive yourself, you automatically forgive all others. Learning forgiveness creates healing in any situation or circumstance.

Forgiveness is empowering and gives you the freedom to move forward in your life. This gives you the freedom to make clear choices based on the present moment and not on the past or the future. Without forgiveness, you will remain stuck in the past, hoping for the future to be different, yet unable to live in the present moment. This will cause you to continue to repeat the same mistakes and errors by drawing to yourself the same types of situations.

Forgiveness is difficult and challenging when you have been personally violated, be it mental or physical. All of us have done things we are not proud of, and know of many things we wish we had not done or said. Each of us has been hurt and each of us has knowingly caused harm to ourselves and others. Forgiveness is realizing we are responsible for our lives.

Forgiveness allows you to free yourself from the negative energy and remove resentments, regrets, bitterness, anger, and fear. Forgiveness does not mean you approve, condone, or even agree with what took place. You do not need to embrace or become friends with anyone as a result. You simply need to remove the negative energy from your life through compassion, humility, and learning.

Detachment is helpful when learning forgiveness. Detaching from any situation is to release the personal and emotional attachments so you can see the situation more clearly, with humility and compassion. Even seeing a situation clearly does not mean you will always understand why something happened. When you don't understand, release the negative energy to God and the Universe so you can move forward. Many times the answers and understanding will come later due to other life experiences. This will usually occur when you least expect it.

Forgiveness is the ability to change your thoughts, emotions, and feelings. This does not mean you erase the memory, but you release the negative energy. It is similar to what happens when a cut heals. You no longer have the cut, but you have the scar.

When you forgive all that happens in your life as it happens, you will no longer feel harmed or carry resentments. This does not mean you should not remove yourself from a situation, or you should consider any part of what happened acceptable. You may even be angry, upset, and hate what happened. However, when you do not release negative energy, you become bound to it and it becomes part of you. Release and let go the negative energy so you will not draw more toward you.

Forgiveness is one of life's most difficult lessons. Until you forgive yourself, you will not forgive others. When you do not forgive yourself, you are actually punishing yourself. Forgiveness removes blame, since actually no one is to blame. Realize no matter what the situation is, you were drawn to it by your energy, not to be punished, but to learn.

When you realize your life's situations, mistakes, errors, and circumstances are about what you came here to learn, you will be able to learn forgiveness. Forgiveness is a way of repenting and atoning. This occurs when you learn the lessons of the situation or circumstance and forgive. This is when forgiveness liberates, frees, and creates positive energy.

When you forgive yourself, you will no longer feel like a victim, feel sorry for yourself, or live in the pain of the past. You will no longer see the world as a bad place where external forces cause your problems. The "Why me?" will turn into "*How* and *what* can I learn from this experience?" The answers will not always come immediately and some answers will come at a later time. Many times the lessons will seem abstract on the surface as to the real *cause* of the situation. As humans we want to see direct cause and effect, but it rarely works this way.

Learning forgiveness will change your life and the lives of others. Forgiveness is letting go of judgments, letting others be who they are, and letting you be who you are. Forgiveness will not only affect the quality of your life and the lives of others, but you will see all things differently for yourself and the world.

Forgiveness can be a difficult lesson to learn in life. To gain understanding, seek and ask for divine guidance, and allow yourself to see the light of God in all persons and situations. Each of us already has God's love, compassion, and forgiveness. It is up to us to learn love, compassion, and forgiveness for ourselves and others by becoming one with God.

Faith

Faith is love. Faith is realized by discovering the light of God within your soul. Faith is the result of experiencing consciousness. As you grow in consciousness, you will grow in faith.

Faith is more than just believing in God. Faith is not blind acceptance, but *feeling* and *knowing* God's love and his message of the Truth. Faith is love and service to God, yourself, and all mankind and creation. Faith is realizing we are souls first before we are human, we are all one, and without God in our lives, our lives are incomplete. To have faith is to surrender and trust in the divine guidance from God and the Universe.

The challenge to live a conscious life is not a test of faith. The only tests of faith come from doubts, and doubts are created by the ego. It is by your own ego that you are tested, not by God. Faith gives you the courage to ignore the doubts of your ego. Without faith, there is blindness to the presence of God's love within your soul. Faith is the ability to see, feel, and know God's light, love, and positive energy within your soul, and in the souls of all mankind and in all creation. It is through faith that our lives are defined. Faith is the awareness and the knowledge of the Truth within our souls.

6

The Truth of Human Life

The Truth of human life has certain gifts and realities that are true for all mankind. The realities of the Truth of human life are inherently known within our souls. It is our ego that questions and doubts the realities. It is important to keep in mind we are human, the presence of the ego is part of our lives, and each of us is superficial to some degree.

The Truth of Human Life Is:
1. The Gift of Love

2. The Gift of Human Life

3. The Gift of Knowledge of the Truth

4. The Gift of Free Will

5. Each Life Is a Journey With a Purpose

6. Change Is Constant, We Are Not in Control, and Everything Happens For a Reason

7. Each of Us Is Responsible for Our Own Life

8. Each of Us Has Good and Bad Qualities

9. Life's Wake-Up Calls Are Meant to Get Our Attention

10. Human Life Is Temporary

11. God's Unconditional Love and Support

Dealing With the Truth of Human Life

1. Becoming Conscious and Connected to the Truth

2. Reality of the Ego-Based Distortions of the Truth

3. Society and the Truth

4. We Are Here to Learn

The Gift of Love

The gift of love is the greatest gift we receive from God, and his love is the light that shines within our souls. Becoming conscious and aware of the Truth is to become aware of God's love. When you are aware of God's love within your soul, you will embrace life as you learn and grow. Learning love is life's greatest lesson.

Love is the greatest gift we receive and is the greatest gift we give to ourselves and others.

The Gift of Human Life

The gift of human life is a gift each of us has been given for the purpose of the growth of our souls. The gift also includes the will to live and a natural hunger for the growth of the soul.

Many feel if life were a gift then at least it could have come with some sort of guarantee. Human life is a gift, and life is as it is supposed to be. When you see life as a gift, you will embrace every aspect of your life, and learn to love and accept every part of you. The doors to your soul will open, and you will concentrate on the growth of your soul with an underlying positive attitude. This does not mean you will become naïve, or you should see everything as a bed of roses. It is about realizing the realities of human life. Life is a journey about growth as a result of the lessons you learn.

Think of your life as a book and you are the author, or a painting and you are the artist. Make your creation grand. Life has no limits. The only limits are those you create for yourself. Life is an incredible journey when you make the choice to live your best life for the highest and greatest good of yourself and all mankind and creation. Live the gift you have been given, and live with passion.

The Gift of Knowledge of the Truth

The gift of knowledge of the Truth is inherent within each of our souls. The Truth will not come to you by mental reasoning or scientific study. The Truth is exposed as an inner knowing from within your soul. Nothing that you will read or that anyone can tell you is more than you already know from within your soul. Seeking external sources of knowledge are helpful to inspire you to access the knowledge within your soul. Becoming conscious and truly knowing and feeling the knowledge will only come from within your soul.

It is up to each of us to discover the Truth. No one can do this for you. You can receive inspiration, validation, and enhancement from external sources, but the connection and knowing will come from within your soul. Seeking knowledge from exterior sources is important and part of the process, but know you will need to make the connection within your soul.

Once you are inspired and you have the desire to connect with your soul, the Truth will come to you as a feeling and a knowing from within the core of your being, and your journey to become conscious will begin. Prior to this time, your life's experiences will be leading you toward this direction. This is true for all of us. However, for some, no matter what happens, they will ignore all the prodding life gives them. This is okay. We need to honor and accept the life path of everyone, since each path is individual and unique, and our differences are a necessary part of the whole.

The Gift of Free Will

The gift of free will allows you to make your own choices and have your own thoughts. The gift of free will allows you to make mistakes and errors, have successes and failures, so you can learn. Life's experiences are not only about your karma, but also about the free will choices you make. The realization of the gift of free will is to realize you are responsible for your life. You are responsible for the choice to become conscious, discover your true self, express your creativity, live your dreams, fulfill your life's purpose, and live authentically. Free will allows you to change your energy and affect what you attract to your life.

Free will is the freedom to make choices so you can learn and grow. Free will does not mean you are in control of your life or the lives of others. You do not have the free will to choose the outcome of your choices. You are only in control of the choices you make, how you interpret the intuition of your soul, and the divine guidance you receive. You also have the free will to ignore the guidance you receive, the lessons you agreed to learn, and your life's purpose. However, when you ignore your life's purpose, it will not ignore you, and there will be constant reminders. Much of life's unhappiness and frustrations occur when you live unconsciously.

Human life is perfect and it is as it is supposed to be at any given moment. Each of us has the free will to choose to embrace life and see it as a positive experience full of wonderful lessons, even though many of the lessons may appear to be unpleasant. When the unpleasant experiences of life are seen as negative, we affect our lives by drawing toward us more negative experiences. This can prohibit learning the lessons of the unpleasant experiences. When these experiences are seen with an underlying positive attitude of lessons to be learned, there is learning and growth.

Everything that happens in your life starts with you. When you make the decision to become conscious, you, along with God, become co-creators of what happens in your life.

Each Life Is a Journey With a Purpose

Each of us arrives with a purpose to fulfill for this lifetime. This is true for every man, woman, and child born to this planet. The purpose of this lifetime is the reason for this lifetime.

Your life's purpose and the lessons you agree to learn for this lifetime are agreed upon before your soul is placed within your mother's womb. When you are born, all the knowledge you need to travel and complete the journey of your life is within your soul. The knowledge is carried within your soul, but with no memory in your mind. It is up to you to become conscious and connected to your soul, so you can begin to access the knowledge.

Our lives are not random events. Nothing happens by accident. You are born at the right time, to the right family. Your life's purpose is relevant to this lifetime and is in relation to your family, relationships, community, and the world. Your purpose in life is specific, but the path is not. You have the gift of free will to choose the path you take. You have the free will to choose what talents you develop, how you progress on your journey, and in what manner.

Living a life that fulfills your purpose is accomplished by unlocking your creative side. Creativity is the expression of your inner being and is not to be confused with the arts. Creativity can be expressed in anything you do. It is your drive, enthusiasm, desire, and passion for how you live your life. Creativity is developing your talents to create balance and harmony in your life as a result of being connected to your soul. Creativity feeds your soul and gives your life meaning.

Discovering your creativity is a result of becoming conscious. As you become connected with your soul, you will begin to peel away the layers to become who you were meant to be. Your creativity will begin to express itself and you may discover talents you might not even been aware of. You may find yourself going in one direction or several different directions as you grow, change, and evolve to discover your creative self. The more connected you become, the more your creativity will express itself.

Fulfilling your life's purpose is the expression of love. When you are creative, you become passionate about life. Your life and your work will become an expression of who you are. You will feel alive and your life will have a richness that can be found no other way. Fulfilling your life's purpose is part of learning and living the values of the Truth. When you ignore your creative side, your life will feel empty and shallow, as if it is passing you by.

The ego-mind will create obstacles that keep you from learning the values of the Truth and fulfilling your life's purpose. Many fail to realize their life's purpose by waiting for some miraculous event to start the process, or expecting their life's purpose to be something grand and extraordinary based on human values. A purpose may be as simple as being an inspiration to others. You can inspire others just by your actions, how you live your life, through general acts of kindness, or just by the essence of your energy. You may inspire others by being a teacher, mentor, or role model. A teacher can have many appearances and many roles other than being a part of formal education. Living to fulfill your life's purpose is grand and fabulous, no matter what it is. When your life's purpose is being fulfilled, your life will be content, satisfying, and you will feel passionate about the life you are living.

The journey of life and fulfilling your life's purpose is not about the material world that our lives seem to revolve around. Fulfilling your purpose is not about satisfying your ego or proving anything to anyone. Your purpose is about the growth and development of your soul. Your life's purpose is an expression of who you are from within and is not about material successes.

When the life you are living is fulfilling your divine purpose, you will be following the intuition of your soul and divine guidance, whether you are aware of it or not. Your life's purpose is not so much what you are doing, but *how* you are doing it. You have the free will to choose the activities you desire to fulfill your purpose.

We enter this life with different roles to fulfill, and each role is an important part of the whole. We are all one, and we are here to learn and grow collectively. Each of our lives has an effect on the whole, and fulfilling our life's purpose is not only about what it teaches us but also how it affects others. When someone's life is short-lived or when someone is mentally challenged, their life's purpose is more about the others that are affected by their life rather than about themselves.

Each of us is born with the innate desire to fulfill our life's purpose. Your life's purpose will come about automatically when your life is about becoming conscious and connecting with your soul, even if you fail to realize it. All the directions you need to fulfill your life's purpose are within your soul. You do not need to search for what you already have. You just need to become aware of the knowledge within.

Change Is Constant, We Are Not in Control, and Everything Happens For a Reason

Change is one of life's absolutes, and change is one thing you can count on. Change is about learning life's lessons, and one of life's lessons is learning to accept all the changes that come your way and to embrace the flow of life. Change is going to occur no matter what you do, and change will cause you to make decisions, or it will make decisions for you. Living the Truth is understanding change is constant, and this is the awareness of the knowledge you are not in control. Not being in control does not mean you are not responsible for your life.

Learning to deal with change is living in the present moment. Learning to accept and deal with the moment is realizing you are not in control, everything happens for a reason, and you need to learn as your life moves forward. You may feel you are in control of your life and the lives of others, but life will always prove to you otherwise. The parts of your life you can control is *how* you deal with the moments, the choices you make, and the thoughts and feelings you have as a result of the gift of free will. Trying to stop change and be in control of your life, and the lives of others, will only cause frustration and lead to negative results. When you realize you are not in control, you can relax and concentrate on *how* you are living your life.

Everything, absolutely everything, happens for a reason, and nothing happens by chance, accident, or due to random events. Understanding everything happens for a reason is realizing and accepting you chose this life, and you continue to choose what you draw to your life due to your energy and the choices you make. When you accept everything happens for a reason, your priorities and intentions will change, and no matter what happens you will accept the results, knowing you have lessons to learn.

Each of Us Is Responsible for Our Own Life

Each of us has chosen the life we are living. We are responsible for everything that happens in our lives, the karma we brought to this lifetime, the karma we generate during this lifetime, and the energy we allow ourselves to absorb from others. This is not meant to be a harsh reality. Knowing everything happens for a reason, does not mean you will understand everything that happens. Just know, everything that happens is related to learning the values of the Truth.

Being responsible is to realize you are responsible for your karma, energy, words, thoughts, emotions, feelings, choices, intentions, fears, doubts, actions, behaviors, desires, achievements, successes, failures, mistakes, errors, happiness, and sadness, no matter what the cause or what the outside influences have been. You are responsible for your quality of life, your values, priorities, and what you focus on in life. This includes your moral code and integrity. You are responsible for becoming conscious, connecting with your soul, living the Truth, and learning life's lessons. It is this understanding that allows you to surrender, let go, and follow the divine guidance you receive from within.

When you are responsible for your life, you will realize life's mistakes and errors are not about punishment but about learning life's lessons. *Life is fair.* Realizing life is fair is to no longer judge or blame yourself or others for what happens. When you are responsible for your life, you will realize each of us is an individual. You will respect others for who they are and realize each of us needs to make our own decisions and learn our own lessons in life.

The awareness that you are responsible for your life comes from within your soul. When you realize you are responsible for your thoughts, choices, intentions, and actions, and the positive or negative energy created, you will make choices more carefully. Being responsible for your life gives you the freedom to embrace life and realize you are responsible for your own joy, happiness, and sadness.

Being responsible for your life will cause your life to take on a whole new meaning. You will no longer look at life's events the same way. You will become accepting of what comes your way by viewing life's experiences with humility, compassion, and forgiveness so you can learn. You will become an active participant in your life, dealing with the *caus-*

es in your life instead of living as a victim of the *effects*. Being responsible is using your *free will* to discover the life you were meant to live.

Life is not about fate or destiny. When you realize you are responsible for your life, you will realize you are responsible for opening the doors of your soul. Once you begin to open the doors to your soul consciously, your life will change dramatically.

Each of Us Has Good and Bad Qualities

Whether we would like to believe it or not, each of us has good qualities, bad qualities, and the potential for evil qualities. These qualities are part of being human and having an ego. If we did not have these qualities, we would not be here. None of our qualities are the result of some obscure exterior force creating turmoil in our lives. It is from both the good and bad that we learn life's lessons. We need to know the bad to know the good, and the good to know the bad. Each of us has the free will to make our own choices, and each of us inherently knows when we are consciously making choices based on the Truth from within our soul, and when we are unconsciously making choices based on our ego-mind.

The bad and evil that exists in the world is not the result of the devil or Satan creating havoc, or God punishing us. This concept was created by man's ego-mind to explain why bad things happen, and to intimidate and control behavior. It was reasoned that if God loves us so unconditionally, then there must be some other source causing the unpleasant parts of our lives, or that we are being punished for our sins. When we give the unpleasant parts of our lives an identity, it becomes an excuse for us not to be responsible for our lives.

What we consider to be bad behavior is the result of our fears, insecurities, and negative energy. This occurs when the doors to our soul are closed and light is absent. Negative energy has no true power. It only has the power we give it. God is the only power that exists, and the light of God's energy is completely positive. Opening the doors of our souls by becoming conscious, exposes and dissolves the darkness with the light and removes the negative energy.

Negative behavior is a trait of the ego, not of the soul. The ego does not accept responsibility for what happens in life. Have you ever said the devil made me do it, or I don't know why I did what I did? When you are honest with yourself and responsible for your thoughts, choices, intentions, and actions, you will know from within it was your choice all along to do whatever. No one makes you do anything that you do not choose to do, and you are responsible for the choices you make in life and the events you draw to your life due to your karma.

Many times what we describe as evil is the result of mental illness, which our society and the world has little understanding of or compassion for. What we refer to as truly evil people throughout history and in the world today are more than likely individuals suffering from some type of mental illness or psychosis. Mentally balanced and rational people do not commit truly heinous act. Understanding this could help us to deal with and prevent some of the horrible criminal acts that have occurred and are still occurring.

Being responsible is learning to deal with the causes of our behavior. Until we deal with causes of life's situations, there will not be changes in the effects. There will continue to be criminal acts as long as we deal with the effects rather than the cause of the acts. Capital punishment has done little to deter violent crime. This is because we as society deal with the effects and not the causes. Educating and teaching the values of the Truth is the solution. As more people strive to live the values of the Truth, we will begin to deal with the causes instead of the effects, and the energy balance of our lives and the world will change.

Life's Wake-Up Calls Are Meant to Get Our Attention

When the reality of life stares us in the face, we become conscious of what matters. At some point during our life's journey, something will happen that will get our attention and inspire us to search inside ourselves for life's meaning. This may be due to a series of frustrating life events, the failed expectations of life, or the awareness that occurs simply due to aging. The reality of what matters in life does not usually become a focus in our lives until something happens to cause us to stop and ask, "Why am I here?" and "What is life about?"

Many lives are lived caught up in the superficial, material life until a wake-up call forces us to deal with life's realities. Living the superficial life is like being a giftwrapped box. The box is beautifully wrapped, but when you open it, it is empty inside. The wake-up call is discovering your box is empty. When this happens, it is meant to get your attention.

All of us have wake-up calls throughout our lives, and we usually ignore them until we are ready to take notice. The realization usually occurs in a moment. This can occur as a simple comment someone makes, a chance meeting, a birth, a death, an illness, an accident, a tragedy, a near death experience, a realization that your life lacks meaning, a miracle, a spiritual experience, or anything that profoundly affects your life. For some it is the awakening of the knowing that has always been there. For many it is the reality that the job promotion, vacation, new house, marriage, divorce, etc., did not give to their life what they thought they needed. When this happens, we naturally ask ourselves questions about our life's meaning. The realization usually occurs when fulfillment and what matters in life has no real correlation with materialistic values.

When wake-up calls occur, we have various reactions. Adversity in our lives will create awareness, anger, bitterness, or resentment, and many times all of the above. Some become angry, bitter, and/or resentful about the circumstances of their lives and become a victim. Some look to the material world for satisfaction. Many are angry, bitter, and/or resentful for a long while, even years, before awareness occurs. Some will become aware, take stock of their lives, and realize they alone have to fix their lives. They begin the search for consciousness. Know that this is not the most common choice, but it is the only choice that is the solution to living a satisfying life.

Each of us experience many wake-up calls throughout our lives, and more often than not we return to our old, familiar ways, even if our intention is not to do so. If the wake-up call is not enough to force you to change your life or if you are not ready, you will more than likely get back on the same treadmill of life you just fell off of. Changing your life will usually involve taking risks or moving out of the comfort zone of your current life, whether it is actually comfortable or not. Change is always difficult, whether it is positive or negative, and no one changes until they are ready. It requires courage, desire, and determination for anyone to make the choice to change and to live consciously.

Human Life Is Temporary

We live in a culture that is in denial of death. Death of the physical body is one of life's absolutes, and is one of life's greatest fears. The fears are due to the uncertainty of what happens after death, the loss felt when a loved one passes, and the distortions of the Truth created by many religious beliefs. However, death is not the grim reaper; it is only the ego-mind that sees it this way.

Death occurs at the right time and in the right way, whether it is due to age, illness, an accident, or a tragedy. Death is one of life's naturally occurring wake-up calls. No death occurs that is not about the effect it has on everyone that person's life has touched. Our lives are impacted not only by the lives of others but by their deaths as well.

The life of our soul is eternal. If we would embrace this fact, we would live much different lives. We find it hard to have complete faith in the message of the Truth, because we want to know what happens in the afterlife, just to know it is real. Faith is knowing when we leave this earth we are returning home. We do know this deep within our souls, but the ego wants actual physical proof. The afterlife is not something we can see or touch, and science has no way of explaining what happens. Only faith and connecting with your soul will give you the answers you seek.

All souls are equal in death, and each of us leaves this earth the same way. It does not matter whether you are royalty or a pauper. Money does not buy you a more privileged way to pass on. It only provides nicer and more comfortable surrounding, and a more expensive funeral. Material possessions have no true value as far as the soul is concerned. Love is the most valued possession of the soul.

Death seems to always greet us unexpectedly. Even when someone is elderly or terminally ill, death seems unexpected. Just know no matter how it happens, unexpectedly, tragically, quietly, or by accident, no one leaves this earth at the wrong time or the wrong way. No death happens when it is not supposed to. This is why it is so important to strive to live your best life each moment of each day. If you live each day as if it were your last, your priorities will always be in order.

To put your life in perspective, evaluate your time spent on earth as if you were receiving grades. At the time of your physical death, your soul will be returning home with a report card. Did you make the grades you expected by striving to do your best, or did you have to take some incompletes for lack of participation? You will not be punished for any incompletes. You will simply have to repeat and complete the work in another lifetime or on another plane of the universe. Live your life so that when your earthly life ends you will know that you lived your best life. Do not arrive at the end of your life's journey and realize that you have been on a misguided tour directed by your ego.

The fact that human life is temporary is certainly no startling revelation to anyone. We live in denial of death, always looking for ways to lengthen and extend our lives rather than focusing on the quality of our lives and why we are here. Death causes us to pause, take stock of our lives, and reflect on our own mortality. Nothing in this life lasts forever except the soul. Why do we value the desires of the ego, and ignore the soul?

The loss of a loved one is one of our greatest hardships in life, and the emptiness can be overwhelming. Just know your loved one has returned home and is in the best place possible. Grieving a loss is a natural and necessary process to heal and to learn from.

God's Unconditional Love and Support

Know you are loved with the total, unconditional love and support from God and the Universe. The unconditional love and positive energy of God and the Universe are available to assist you and guide you at any time. The help you need will always appear at the right time and in the right way. God and the Universe will not manipulate a situation, but merely point you in the right direction. You will receive clues to guide you on your way, but you have to be aware and listen from within your soul, and then choose the path you take based on your perception of the clues. Know your perception can be influenced by your ego.

The support needed to become conscious is found in the Truth. The knowledge of the Truth is love, and "The Truth will set you free." The best things in life are free, and the Truth is free! Once you realize God is within you, and the knowledge of the Truth is within you, you will be free. The Truth will bring balance and harmony to your life. When you live the Truth, you will be true to yourself and others. The freedom of the Truth will simplify your life, and great wisdom is found in simplicity. Live your life with love, devoted and loyal to God and the Truth, and the path your life follows will amaze you.

Becoming Conscious and Connected to the Truth

Human life is a balance between the unconscious ego-mind and the conscious soul. Balancing the two as you learn can feel like being on a seesaw. Human life is about the journey, not the arrival.

We are not born enlightened, and complete enlightenment is rarely achieved here on earth. If this were possible, there would be many examples of those who had, and the world would be a much different place. The only true examples we have to follow are those of the ascending masters. They were born, just as we are, with their life's path not clearly laid out in front of them. Their lives were far from easy, and they had to become committed and surrender their lives to God to fulfill their purpose. They had to face and deal with many of the trials and tribulations of life just as we do. Their faith was tested due to their own doubts just as ours is. They are more evolved and the purpose of their lives was more exceptional than ours is, but they each had to discover this for themselves. It is up to us to follow their examples as best we can.

Consciousness is a choice that is available for each of us to make. Becoming conscious is a journey that is continuous throughout your entire life. The journey will not always be easy, there will be many twist and turns, highs and lows, but the rewards are the finest you will ever know. Once you become aware of the Truth and feel it within your being, you will be started on your journey. You will never look at life's situations the same way again, and you begin to live the life you were meant to live.

The Truth is something you must realize within yourself by feeling it. When you search outside yourself for the awareness of the Truth, it is like searching for the keys to your car, which have been in your pocket the entire time. Becoming conscious is like finding the keys to your car in your pocket, taking them out, and driving your life. You have to let go of the thoughts of your ego-mind that are causing you to live an unconscious life, and any worldly, material stuff that is blocking you from connecting with your soul. All the knowledge you need is within your soul. You already have it. God, the Universe, and your soul are waiting patiently for you to embrace the awareness and become conscious.

The choice to become conscious and live an authentic life is not easy. If it were easy, everyone would be doing it. Once you start the process, the doors of your soul will open, but be patient and do not force the process. The soul is patient, and the ego is not. If you have the desire and are willing to make the commitment, the answers and guidance you need will appear.

Reality of the Ego-Based Distortions of the Truth

The simple message of the Truth has become distorted with nontruths, misinterpretations, and contradictions due to man's ego. Mankind has come to believe the distortions created by the ego out of habit and traditions. It is man that has complicated the Truth of God's message. As a result, the Truth is seen as complicated and abstract, like most would view calculus, instead of the reality of its simplicity, like simple math a+b=c. The Truth is basic, pure, consistent, universal, timeless, and uncomplicated.

Honesty and what is true exposes all nontruths in any situation. When something is true, there are no secrets, lies, deceit, or distortions. That which is a nontruth is inconsistent, distorted, dishonest, false, destructive, and is negative energy and darkness. Any omission of what is true is still a nontruth, and a nontruth will contaminate any situation. Be aware that the ego-mind is capable of believing anything. In any situation, reject all nontruths and any distortions of the Truth that you feel from within your soul. Accept nothing less than the Truth from any teachings.

Your soul knows the difference between what is true and false, but your ego does not. You inherently know when you are lying and when you are being lied to. You also know when someone is intentionally causing you harm and when you are intentionally causing harm to yourself or others. You are also aware of when you are being honest and truthful and when you are not. Always adhere to the Truth and what is honest and true as it applies to your life. Focus on the values of the Truth as you deal with life.

The message of the Truth teaches we are all one, created equal and loved by God unconditionally, and we do not have the ability to judge one another. Be committed to the Truth of God's message on your own terms, no one else's, based on your soul's knowledge of the Truth. Do not use the Truth or any other reasoning to judge others. Do not look down upon or judge others who do not have the same vision or see the Truth as you do. Respect each person's level of consciousness and path in life, since judgments are the result of our ego and we do not have the ability or the knowledge to judge anyone's life.

Society and the Truth

Our society and our culture do not openly embrace a spiritually conscious life. The focus of society is not on the values of the Truth and this makes living the Truth difficult. To live the Truth you have to be willing to become an individual and not one of society's puppets. You must be willing to give up any of the materialistic human values that keep you from living the values of the Truth, following your inner voice, living your beliefs, and being true to your soul.

Why is living the Truth not the norm? Why is discussing the Truth and God a controversial topic? Why do we fear God's wonderful message of the Truth? Why have we allowed the distortion of the Truth to affect our lives, when each of us has the knowledge of the Truth within our souls? Why is it so difficult to connect with our souls? Why is it so difficult to discover our purpose in life? Why do we wonder why we are here? Why are none of these questions openly discussed or addressed? Why do we fail to realize the Truth is universal, timeless, and it unites all mankind and all faiths? The answer is we live our lives on the surface, from the ego's point of view, and not from the soul's. Living the Truth is in conflict with our egos and the lifestyle of our society and the world. Our focus is more on the superficial, material life than on what matters. We have the illusion that living a material life will bring us happiness and inner peace. We look outside ourselves for the answers when the answers are within each of us. The answer is to become conscious, connected to our souls, and strive to live the values of the Truth.

We Are Here to Learn

Life is not a game; it is a journey, and we are here to learn. We have lost the concept of what the values of the Truth mean. We see love as need, and integrity as me first. We see compassion as pity, and we put Band-Aids on cuts that need to be stitched. We see forgiveness as justice, with no consideration for the cause or the lessons to be learned. We see peace as the resolution of conflict. We lack individuality due to the lack of self-esteem. We live with conflict, confusion, unhappiness, and the attitude that life is not fair. Our life's experiences are constant wake-up calls about the lessons we are here to learn. We function best together when we are individuals with self-esteem. This creates balance and harmony.

Learning the values of the Truth is why we are here. Success in life is learning and striving to live the values of the Truth. Realizing this will change our world. Do not be frustrated with those who do not want to learn. It is the few who will take on the challenge to become conscious, and it is the few who will make a difference for all mankind.

7

Senses of the Soul

We live in a world that is mainly focused on the physical and material aspects of life. As humans, we rely on five senses to function in our physical lives. We take these five senses for granted unless one or more of them is missing. We rely on and easily believe in anything we can physically see, touch, taste, smell, and/or hear. We have additional senses that are the nonphysical senses of the soul. The senses of the soul deal with the nonphysical, spiritual part of our being. The nonphysical senses of our being are just as important to living a full and productive life as the physical senses.

The senses of the soul are *the intuition of the soul, the inherent knowledge of the Truth, and the innate hunger for our oneness with God.* The senses of our soul are within each of us. The awareness of the senses of your soul is the result of quieting your mind, becoming conscious, and connecting to your soul. Developing the senses of the soul requires not only awareness, but also desire. Becoming aware of the senses of your soul is a choice only you can make for yourself.

The Intuition of Your Soul
The intuition of your soul is the navigator of your life's

journey. Intuition is your soul's way of communicating with you to guide you through life. This is the inner voice of your higher self. Intuition will come to you as a knowing that you will *feel* from within your soul. The intuition of the soul is the gateway to the knowledge of the meaning of your thoughts, emotions, and feelings, and to the knowledge to discover their cause. The intuition of your soul is your guide to learning life's lessons.

Intuition comes from the knowledge you have within your soul and the divine guidance you receive, which is the guidance from God and the Universe. Intuition is a feeling that may be in the form of a thought, a hunch, a feeling in your gut, or that little voice inside you. It may also come to you in many different ways such as a vision or dream, a comment or conversation, something you read or watch, or anything that stirs a feeling deep within your being. The signs that trigger your intuition can come from just about anywhere. There are no coincidences or accidents in life. Trust your intuition and it will never fail you. Your intuition will guide you to live your dreams, your best life, and your authentic life.

The intuition of the soul comes from within your soul, but it can also appear a false illusion from your ego-mind. The intuition of the soul is subtle, but the effect it has on you can be overwhelming as well as humbling. The intuition you receive from your soul will be definite and based on the values of the Truth. The false illusion of intuition that comes from your ego will be dominating, controlling, and associated with the wants and needs of the material life. The intuition of your soul will give you more wisdom and information about your life than your ego-mind or intellect can imagine. It will take practice to not confuse the intuition of your soul with the wants and needs of your ego. Trust what is within your soul and realize the role of your ego. Following the intuition of your soul will silence your ego and create change in your life.

We live in a complicated society that takes little time for

one's self, and going, doing, and being seems to run our lives, leaving us unable to focus on what really matters in life. Getting in touch with our souls is not a common practice, and as a result we have become spiritually starved and hungry for consciousness.

People who are not connected to their souls or in touch with their feelings are not comfortable around those that are. It causes them to think about having to deal with their own lives, and this is something many would rather not do. When we do not deal with our lives from within, life becomes frustrating and stressful as a result. It is like being on a sailboat without a sail.

Being conscious of your feelings and connecting with your soul can be intimidating and uncomfortable when you first begin. Going deep within and being honest with yourself can be difficult due to the involvement of your ego. When you connect with your true feelings, you may find what you are feeling is upsetting. This is because of the awareness you really knew what your true feelings were all along, but you suppressed them, ignored them, or did not want to face them. Facing your true feelings is not about shame, guilt, or punishment. Facing your true feelings means dealing with your life so you are able to learn life's lessons.

As you become conscious, you will need to learn to trust your intuition, have faith, and live a life that supports a conscious lifestyle by striving to live the values of the Truth. This will require you to become an individual. As an individual you will become centered, relying on your intuition and doing what is right for you by being true to yourself. When you are in touch with and conscious of your intuition, you will be following your inner guidance to find meaning and satisfaction in life. When you are not an individual or secure within yourself, you will seek the approval of others and will be affected by what others think. This will influence how you react to your intuition and may leave you feeling misguided. When you suppress or ignore your intuition, you will misinterpret what you feel, and your ego will be in control of your life.

Getting in touch with your intuition will affect your life and how you feel about yourself. You will begin to take time for yourself, your priorities will change, and you will simplify your life by removing issues that keep you from being who you really are. You will remove from your life those things that no longer align with your integrity, and do not feed your soul. Removing the excess clutter in your life will allow you to focus on you. Simplifying your life externally will make it easier to simplify it internally. When you allow yourself to feel from within your soul, you will know what you are doing is right for you. Your inner feeling of satisfaction, contentment, and happiness will indicate to you that your life is flowing in the right direction.

Learning to follow your intuition is a process that will not take place overnight. It is a process that will take practice and patience. The fears of your ego will surface from time to time creating doubt, no matter how connected you think you are. Dealing with doubt and insecurities created by your ego is part of the learning process. Do not let this concern or stop you, since our lives are a continuous work in progress. Move at your own pace with desire, commitment, and determination, relying on your inner guidance. When you arrive at a fork in the road of life, listen to your intuition and follow the path your soul wants to take.

Learning to follow your intuition when you start to connect with your soul will take you out of the comfort zone of your ego. Be patient, loving, compassionate, and forgiving with yourself. Part of the process is learning to recognize the difference between the intuition of your soul and the needs of your ego, and this is not always easy. Do what feels right, even if you would normally question it. When something does not feel right, detach from the situation to see it more clearly, or do nothing.

Accept your intuition at face value. Anytime you try to influence or change your intuition, the interpretation will become misguided. When you receive messages from your soul, the guidance will be a definite do or don't and will align with the values of the Truth. The messages you receive from your ego create doubt and raise the questions of maybe, but, what if, what for, why, when, where, why not, should I, shouldn't I, etc.

You will not always interpret your intuition the way it was intended, even when you are aware of the influences of your ego. You will still make mistakes and errors in judgment. Do not see this as a negative, but see it as part of learning process. Take the time to reflect and understand it was your misinterpretation, caused by your ego, stress, worry, doubt, not trusting yourself, or any number of outside influences, not the intuition of your soul. Your intuition will never fail you. It is you who will misunderstand and misinterpret it. Be patient and allow yourself the time to learn, and you will realize you are never misguided by the intuition of your soul.

Your intuition will guide you in a direction, but it will not explain the details or make the choices for you. You have the free will to choose the path you take. When you follow your intuition and everything works out the way you wanted it to, you feel happy and guided. However, there will be times when you follow your intuition and everything will seem to fall apart, and you will feel unhappy and misguided. When this happens do not become discouraged; stay positive, detach, and learn. The results of the guidance you receive may not be what you expect, but the results will be what you need as part of the learning process. You will not always understand or get the directions and answers you want, but you will get the directions and answers you need. Keep moving forward, knowing things will work out as they should, and realize all situations have a positive outcome when your intentions are based on the values of the Truth and learning life's lessons.

When things do not work out as desired, ask yourself some questions. "What was I really thinking or trying to accomplish?" "What part of my decision was based on the wants and needs of my ego or outside influences?" "What were my intentions?" "What did I not allow myself to feel?" What feelings do I need to deal with?" "Was I being true to myself?" And most importantly ask, "What lessons do I need to learn, or what lessons did I just learn?"

When you are trying to understand what your intuition is telling you, be honest with yourself and you will know when you are following your intuition or when you are adjusting it to fit your ego's wants and needs. When you allow your ego or others to influence you, you give away your power. When you accept it was your choice to relinquish your power, you can take back your power by ignoring the influences of your ego and others.

There will also be times when you are not ready to deal with what your intuition is telling you, even though you know what you are feeling is right. Don't be upset with yourself when you know you should have listened to your intuition. This is part of the learning process. You will know when you need to make a change in your life and when your fears are holding you back. After you make the change, take time to reflect and feel what held you back. This is a great time to learn more about yourself and to realize things happen for a reason.

Intuition will not make your choices for you. You have to be willing to take the risks and trust in yourself. You must be willing to accept the outcome, knowing there are no right or wrong choices, just choices to learn from. When you deny your feelings, lack faith and trust in yourself, and fear making the wrong decision or choice, your ego will be involved and you will be setting up roadblocks and obstacles to your intuition.

Intuition is not about always knowing the right thing to do so your life will be perfect. Life is about learning the lessons necessary for the growth of your soul. By becoming conscious, you will accept what happens in your life, knowing it happened for a reason, and that you are responsible for the path you are on. When you practice following your intuition without bias or doubt, you will feel good about your life without question. Your intuition will give you the answers you are looking for. As you become more aware and connected, your intuition will become clearer and freer from negative influences.

The intuition of your soul is helpful in all areas of your life. Your intuition will keep you safe by letting you know when you are uneasy about a situation. The intuition of your soul will serve as inspiration in your life by giving you insight into your creativity and guiding you to your purpose in life. It will help you to take the proper turns, read the right books, take the right classes, and meet the right people necessary to open the doors of your soul. Learning to let the intuition of your soul guide your life is the key to a satisfying life.

The Inherent Knowledge of the Truth

The knowledge of the Truth is within the soul of each and every one of us. No one is born without it. The purpose of human life is to become aware of the knowledge within the soul. Awareness of that knowledge leads to growth of the soul.

This knowledge of the Truth is deep within your soul and cannot be found on the surface of your life. To become aware of this knowledge, it is necessary to access it. Even being aware of a small amount has the ability to significantly change your life. Once you tap into this knowledge, you will no long accept any nontruths that do not align with what you feel from within your inner knowing of the Truth.

The Innate Hunger for Our Oneness With God

Each of us is born with the natural hunger to become conscious and connected to our oneness with God. Actually, the connection is already there. The light of God's love is within each of our souls. It is just up to us to become aware of it.

Our superficial unconscious lives have left us selfless and spiritually starved. The hunger is evident in our stressful and complicated lives. The hunger is what causes us to search for the meaning of our lives. The reason we are here is for the growth of our souls. True satisfaction and meaning in life does not occur without the connection to our souls and the oneness with God.

Part 3

8

Religion

Religion is often confused with spirituality; many consider the two to be the same, but the two are actually very different. Many think anything that is spiritual, or has to do with God, is also religious. Religion is not a requirement to having a strong belief and devotion to God. A spiritual life does not require the involvement of religion. You can be both religious and spiritual at the same time; however, being religious is not necessarily being spiritual. You do not have to be religious to invite God into your life or to have him be a part of your life. Being religious or spiritual will not connect you with God unless you make the connection from within your soul. Having God in your life comes from within, no matter whether you are religious or not.

The belief in a higher power has been documented back as far as the beginning of mankind, and all faiths and religions have common roots that can be found in the Truth. When asked, most would acknowledge a higher power is responsible for our existence. Why is it we ignore the existence of a higher power (God) by not involving the source (God) in our daily lives, when the source (God) is the very reason for our existence?

Religious principles, rules, and doctrines have been taught

and practiced for centuries, and freedom from principles, rules, and doctrines have been sought for centuries as well. Distortions and misinterpretations have evolved over time due to man's ego and the quest to solve the mystery of the Truth. The Truth is not a mystery, but our ego tells us it is.

The distortions creating the mysteries of the Truth have been created and taught based on man's way of thinking, and not God's message. Due to involvement of the ego, man sees a minimum of two sides to every story. It is our ego that makes interpretations to fit its needs. God's message of the Truth has only one side, and it is positive and inspirational. If we would go back to the basics of the Truth and practice teaching the Truth as taught by the ascending masters, nontruths would be exposed and no longer practiced.

We live in a society where religion and spirituality are not openly embraced. We deal with God and our faith on an as-needed basis. We thank God for our good fortune and question God when unfortunate events occur. We ask for help when in need and once the situation has been resolved, we forget about God until the next time we are in need.

A general attitude of negativity surrounds both religion and spirituality, due to past oppressive religious practices, that have dominated beliefs for hundreds of years. Many of these practices and beliefs have not provided real support or given the answers we need. It has been man's ego that has created nontruths and distortions resulting in negative attitudes, not God's message of the Truth. It is our souls and not our egos that recognize the Truth. It is connecting with our souls that will change our lives, change the practice of religious faiths as we know them today, and change the world.

All religions have had very true beginnings, but many have lost the meaning of the Truth over time. The Truth has become distorted, causing religion to lose sight of what is really important, resulting in the religion becoming more important to itself than the Truth. This is not the fault of the religion, but the misguided intentions of the egos of those who created the distortions. The early religious leaders and rulers were totalitarian and authoritarian in nature, and they developed many of the religious doctrines still taught today. Those rulers, by their nature, did not want anyone thinking outside the box. They expected their rules, regulations, and doctrines to be followed by blind faith simply because they said it was so; actually, because they demanded it. Some were truly committed to what they believed to be true, and others created rules for the underlying purpose of gaining power and control over the people. Even with the best intentions, religious practices, rules, and regulations throughout history have been affected by politics, culture, and desires of the various leaders. This has led to many nontruths being practiced as traditions, rituals, and habits that have lasted many hundreds of years.

The teachings of religious faiths tend to be more about the practice of their rules, rather than about *how* to live life according to the values of the Truth. Many times the rules and regulations have nothing to do with the Truth. When you practice a religious faith, it is assumed that *how* you live your life is based on its rules and regulations, but this is not always the case. There is usually a division between everyday life and practice of one's faith. Seldom are lives lived following the rules of a faith, or lived based on the Truth.

The examples I am most familiar with are related to the Catholic faith, since this is my background. These are simple examples, but they are representative of how rules have nothing to do with the Truth. When I was a small child having to eat fish on Fridays was a rule. This made no sense to me. I did not understand how eating fish affected anything, and besides I did not like fish. I knew God loved me, and if he had wanted me to eat fish on Friday, he would have at least had me like it. I knew eating fish had nothing to do with God's love or having faith in him. Then, some years later and much to my delight, this rule was changed. This only caused me to further question the rules and teachings of the Church. I wondered, if this was God's rule, then how could the church just decide to change it?

There also was the requirement of going to mass every Sunday. It was taught that if you went to mass every Sunday, you would go to heaven. Going to mass on a regular basis has no real value unless you consider it an important part of your being conscious. It is living the values of the Truth that matters whether you attend church or not.

The requirement of tithing has nothing to do with the Truth. Tithing does not buy you God's love or approval. Tithing to support the institution of your faith is one thing, but the accumulation of wealth by many religious faiths is another. The Truth has nothing to do with money.

Today, we are in a great time of change for the religions of the world. Many of the rules and doctrines that are no longer relevant are beginning to change. Some of the old habits, views, and traditions that are negative are being released, with more emphasis on teaching the Truth. Those who are seeking the Truth and a meaning for life want the message to be positive and relevant. This is the reason for the growing popularity in nondenominational church groups, and a combining of eastern and western philosophies. People are seeking a positive message and enhancement for their lives.

Religious faiths are important and have had a dramatic effect on the history of the world. Religions have played, and continue to play, a very important role in the lives of many. Many are drawn to a religious faith in search of guidance and to find meaning in life. Religions give us a source to hear God's message, start us on our journey, and give us a place to worship with a sense of belonging and community.

The religions of the world can and do have a great deal of influence on the lives of many. All religious faiths are the same in their foundation. If the various religions would honor and practice the Truth, which is at the base of each of their foundations, the religious faiths of the world would flourish and all mankind would benefit. We can learn a great deal by realizing how similar the different faiths are. The reality is we are all the same and the Truth is the same for all faiths. It is up to us to realize this and create harmony in the world.

The Golden Rule is at the foundation of all religious faiths, further emphasizing the message of the Truth. The ascending masters taught the Golden Rule in its true form. It is man's ego that has betrayed the teachings with distortions and prejudiced attitudes about others. Religious faiths teach the values of the Truth, but at the same time create conflict in the teaching by supporting the negative values of guilt, shame, prejudice, intolerance, judgment, capital punishment, and war. How can there be support for the two opposing sides? As humans, we are able to feel both love and fear (hate), so we think this is how God sees things as well. God is love and positive energy exclusively. The contradictions are justified by the ego-mind, but not by the soul or by God's message of the Truth.

The Golden Rule guides us to have reverence for life, and accept ourselves and others. This practice is not common in the world today. Why is it so difficult for us to live by the Golden Rule? Why is it we think all faiths are so different, when the ascending masters taught God's message of the Truth? Why do Christians think their God is the only true God, and any God of a non-Christian faith is false? The belief in a higher power as the source of our existence is the belief in the same God, no matter what name is used. It is man's ego and not God's message that has created the misunderstandings.

The teachings of God's message of the Truth were not meant to be a source of conflict, punishment, or judgment, under any circumstances. We need to discard the negative teachings, rules, and doctrines that are meant to control and judge others. They promote conflict, fear, punishment, shame, and guilt. Just because practices have been handed down and taught for hundreds of years does not make them right.

God, our creator, is the God of all religions. Since God is

the God of all mankind, does it really matter what religion or faith someone follows? God is available to be an active part of everyone's life, regardless of their faith or lack of faith. What is important is how we live our lives. Living the Truth is not about practicing a religious faith. Living the Truth is living the values of the Truth and becoming one with God, no matter what faith is being practiced.

In the past and still today, leaders of religions, faiths, and philosophies have instituted rules and regulations for the purpose of power, control, the glamour of leadership, and financial gain. Many of these rules and regulations are meant to affect the behavior and self-esteem of the congregation for the purpose of creating loyalty. This has resulted in the baggage associated with many faiths over the years, causing many to have unpleasant experiences associated with religious practices and teachings. It is not that the religions should be considered bad or wrong, it is just what has happened due to man's ego being involved in the process. Any time money, power, control, and ego are involved in any practice, you can be certain God's message of the Truth is not a priority.

Religious beliefs have been a source of conflict throughout history. Distortions of the Truth have created a basis for judgment that has divided populations and created conflict between religious groups. Religion has been blamed for many of the wars fought throughout history. But it is more than just religious beliefs, it is man's ego seeking power and control, and the fears and distortions of the Truth that have caused conflicts and wars. In the medieval times of crusades and holy wars, there was an obsession with sin. To create large armies, the concept was created that to fight and/or die would serve for complete remission of sin. The offer was made to all creating many devout warriors. The result was a blood thirst for war that lasted hundreds of years. The crusades took place to force the gospel upon others, and to gain land and power for the bishops, popes, kings, and emperors. This created the misconception that to fight and die in war is honorable, a belief still held today. The topic of religion raises emotions in most everyone. Having a conversation with someone about religion is like having a discussion about politics. No one can agree and sides are usually chosen. Religion has continued to divide people through the ages, while the message of the Truth is meant to unite us. What we do not understand and what is not familiar, we usually choose not to accept. One faith is so quick to judge another, believing theirs is more right, more important, more true, and in some way they are God's chosen group. All of this is due to the influences of the ego.

When I have a conversation with someone about God and Christian religious beliefs, several issues always come up that create controversy. The first is that we are not worthy of God's love and should fear the wrath of God because we are sinners. The second is, was Jesus Christ conceived by Immaculate Conception? The third is the confusion about how different faiths interpret the Bible.

Are We Sinners?

No! We are *not* sinners and we are *not* born sinners. Jesus Christ did not die on the cross to save us from our sins. If Jesus Christ died for our sins, then why would we still consider ourselves sinners? How could Jesus have died for our sins, if he rose from the dead?

God loves us unconditionally. Our lives on this earth have nothing to do with being punished for our sins by God. Each of us is born with the karma we bring and a purpose for this lifetime. Human life is about learning the lessons we need for the growth and development of our soul on our journey toward enlightenment.

It is taught that sin is displeasing and disrespectful to God, and you must repent and/or be punished, with the ultimate punishment being hell. Sin has been associated with evil, fear, guilt, and shame, and has been used as a means of control by holding heaven and hell over the heads of many. As a result, sin has become an obsession for many religious faiths. The concepts of sin, punishment, and hell were created due to fears and misunderstandings of God's message, and relating it to man's way of thinking. The concept of sin has served as a basis for power, control, judgment, humiliation, and intimidation.

Sin has been a source of oppression, guilt, and shame for thousands of years. Sin and its negative associations have been used to create value judgments about right and wrong, good and bad. Sin, along with guilt and shame, are words I wish could be removed from our vocabulary. Not because of the words, but because of the negative meanings and associations they carry. Sins are nothing more than mistakes and errors we make as part of life's journey to learn life's lessons. Mistakes and errors are not about being right or wrong, or good or bad. We are human and are supposed to make mistakes and errors for the purpose of learning life's lessons resulting in the growth of our souls. Life is about learning and growth, not about being sinners.

We do not anger God with what is referred to as sin. God's love for us is pure, unconditional positive energy, and each and every one of us is worthy of God's love. There is no wrath of God to fear. God is not about judgment, intimidation, punishment, rules, or regulations. These are the misguided teachings of the ego. Man's ego rationalizes that God must think and feel the same way we do. God's way of thinking is not equivalent with ours and God does not have an ego. God's love is unconditional and God loves us more than any of us can imagine. God knows absolutely everything about each of us, why we are here, and what purpose we are to fulfill. God created us and he sees the big picture of our lives, while mankind only sees snapshots.

God does not set traps for us to fall into. We are responsible for our lives, and we have the free will to make choices.

Each of us is responsible for setting our own traps by the choices we make, the thoughts we have, the karma we brought to this lifetime, and the karma we create during this life. It is in accepting responsibility for our thoughts and choices that the journey of learning life's lessons begins.

Conceived by Immaculate Conception?

The Immaculate Conception of Jesus has been questioned by many. Many have gotten hung up on the issue of his birth. Was Jesus Christ conceived by Immaculate Conception? It is God who gives us life in human form, and it is God who places our souls within the womb of our mothers. It was God who placed the soul of Jesus within Mary, no matter how he was conceived. So, yes he was conceived by Immaculate Conception.

Was Mary a virgin? What did the term virgin mean two thousand years ago? History indicates the word "virgin" meant a young woman of childbearing age or a young woman who was carrying her first child. The term immaculate was used to mean free of original sin, and therefore, gave purity to the birth. The concept of original sin was created by man, not by God.

Would it really matter if Mary was a virgin or not? Would it matter whether Jesus Christ was conceived by Immaculate Conception or not? Would it make Christ's life any less valid or important? Would we believe his message any more or any less? Would this cause us to deny the miracles he performed or that he rose from the dead? The purpose of Jesus Christ's birth was that while his life was extraordinary, he still lived a human existence just like the rest of us, not only to teach us God's message of the Truth, but to serve as an example for us to live by.

When you stop and think about it, all mankind is and has been conceived by Immaculate Conception. It is by God's creation that we exist. Our conception and birth are not the result of random events. The conception of human life is due to God's creation, not man's. We are born to the right family, at the right time, and with a purpose for this lifetime. God is the creator of our lives and he is responsible for giving us the gift of life. How we are conceived in human terms is not relevant.

The Bible

The Bible is one of the most widely read books of all times. The meaning of the word "gospel" is good news. How can there be negative and harmful messages if the intention of the gospels were meant to be the good news of God's message? Why are there so many versions, translations, and misunderstandings of the Bible? The gospels and scriptures were meant to be messages of good news to teach us the values of the Truth and faith, not guilt, shame, punishment, or judgment.

Man has used the Bible to cause as much harm as good by justifying the wants and needs of the ego. Man has used the Bible for the judgment of others, to cause shame and guilt, and to defend reasons for punishment and war. Jesus, as God's messenger, did not ridicule, attack, or harm anyone, yet we use the Bible to do just that. We cannot have it both ways. This was not the intention of God's message. God's message was intended to be completely positive and inspirational, and to give us examples to live by. The stories were meant to be symbolic, to guide us on life's journey, and to help us learn life's lessons.

The Bible is and has been controversial. The Bible has been translated, interpreted, and rewritten many times since the original. We do not have the original to know what it actually said. Everyone perceives and interprets happenings and events differently, and this naturally depends on one's point of reference, level of consciousness, cultural background, intentions, life experiences, etc. The purpose of many of the translations has been to fit the personal needs of different leaders, and to gain power and control of a general population or group. This is no different than the way things are done today. We twist words, statistics, and reports to fit our hidden agendas and to support our wants and needs.

The contents of the Old and New Testaments are results of selections made by various leaders, and we have no idea what deletions, additions, or changes occurred. The New Testament was composed of the four selected works of Matthew, Mark, Luke, and John, plus the letters from Paul. Irenaeus, bishop of Lyons, in approximately the year 180, chose the works for the New Testament and in doing so discarded other works that existed at that time. History indicates he did this for the purpose of unity. The Roman Emperor Constantine, in approximately 325, brought all the bishops together to canonize the contents of the New Testament. The cost of having scribes write the New Testament as one text was expensive and had not been done up to this time. Constantine had the resources and paid for the writing. This also put him in charge of the final composition and the duplicates that were made.

The writing of the works chosen for the New Testament did not begin until approximately 40 years after the death of Christ. These were not an exact transcription of Christ's words. Paul's letters were some of the earliest writings. Paul was not a disciple, but he was well acquainted with Jesus and spent a great deal of time with him discussing God's message. Mark's writings, considered to be among the first, took place around the years 65-75. But Mark was a small child at the time of Jesus' death and was thought to be a disciple of Peter. Luke, a companion of Paul, was not even born while Jesus was alive. His writings occurred around the years 80-95. Matthew and John were disciples of Jesus, but their writings did not occur until years 75-85, and 90-95, respectively. This places their ages, at the time of their writings, well past the average life expectancy of the times. This raises some questions as to whom the actual authors were. Authorship was not claimed within any of the texts.

The Bible reflects confusion about Jesus' message and disagreements among the writers. It is also important to note that much of the writing took place in a very turbulent time during the establishment of Christianity. Keep in mind that the year 70 was when the Romans destroyed the Temple and much of Jerusalem.

The original texts were written in Aramaic. Then were translated into Greek, then Latin, prior to the translation into English. Aramaic is an ancient, simple language with the exact meanings of some phrases difficult to translate. Were any of the meanings misinterpreted, taken out of context, or misunderstood? Even today, it is very hard to translate one language exactly to another, and it must also be realized the meanings of some words and phrases change over time. Just think how many different meanings and interpretations there are for words in the English language and how they have changed over time. In addition, a direct translation is not always possible for every concept, and information is always lost or gained in any translation. We must also consider the variables of the mindset and level of consciousness of the translators.

Many of the teachings that occurred two thousand years ago were in the form of parables and were meant to be symbolic. Would a story told two thousand years ago have the same frame of reference or meaning today? What part of the scriptures actually happened, and what parts were meant to be examples in the form of stories, parables, fables, analogies, or metaphors that have since been given a literal translation? Everyone hears, sees, and interprets things differently. This has been proven with witnesses to crimes. Think back ten, twenty, thirty, or forty years. How clear is your memory of exact events in your life? How have your life events changed in your memory? On the surface you may think your memory is accurate, but try to pinpoint the exact details of an event that occurred some twenty years ago. Not that the original writings were not true, but we do not have an actual accounting of Christ's words.

The Bible is full of symbolism that has been and continues to be interpreted many different ways. When interpreting God's message of the Truth, the only possible way to interpret it is to align the symbolism with the values of the Truth. Truthful interpretations are of the soul, and false and misleading interpretations are of the ego. Some of the stories have been interpreted based on man's ego with the intent to create desired effects for the means of power and control, and this has created false and misleading interpretations.

An example of how interpretation has caused confusion is the Ten Commandments. When I was in the second grade, we were taught the Ten Commandments. I was upset that we were being taught to follow them as God's rules to live by, knowing they were not being supported or practiced. For example, Thou shall not kill. We were taught that to kill someone was a mortal sin and a ticket to hell. I knew wars were being fought and there was support from the Church. I knew there was nothing in God's message or in his love that supported war. I also knew the explanation of false gods was not true. God abandons no one, even if their beliefs are not Christian. False gods are the material gods of man's ego. I knew other commandments were not being followed, but there was the pretense that they were.

The story of Adam and Eve is an example of symbolism, as many of the gospels were meant to be. Whether the story is true or not, it is the symbolism of the message that is important. The story tells us we are all one, and we have been given the gift of life and free will. Adam and Eve were given the gift of life, the gift of free will, and this beautiful world referred to as paradise. God explained to them the message of the Truth. The temptation of Eve, followed by her influencing Adam, shows us that when we do not live by the values of the Truth and we allow temptations to enter our lives (the wants and needs of the ego, and outside influences), our lives become difficult and misguided. This also demonstrates to us that we are responsible for our actions, choices, and intentions, and that we inherently know from within our being when the choices align with the Truth, and when they do not. When we live with love, honor, and respect for ourselves and others, the world is a paradise and life is beautiful. Life becomes difficult when we do not.

Isn't it interesting how the teachings of Jesus Christ were controversial and misunderstood during his time on earth, and the controversy and misunderstandings continue still today? Why are there so many misunderstandings of Jesus Christ's wonderful message? Why are the gospels of Matthew, Mark, Luke, and John similar, yet contradictory? Why do we have so many interpretations, and why are many of the messages interpreted as negative and threatening? We need to realize the good of God's message, instead of twisting it to fit the needs of the ego.

If we did have the original writings of the Bible, how accurate would today's translations be? Why does the Bible leave us with so many questions? Everything happens for a reason. The reason for so much confusion where the Bible is concerned is that we do not rely on our inner knowing of the Truth. The Truth is revealed to us if we quiet our minds and go deep within our souls. What is important is that we *do* have the knowledge and the proof of God's message within our souls. Each of us inherently knows the Truth, and becoming conscious is the key to accessing our knowledge of the Truth.

All messages from God are positive. All messages from God reflect the values of the Truth, or describe life's lessons as related to the values of the Truth. Any interpretations, other than these values are nontruths due to the influence of man's ego. God's messages are not about shame, guilt, or punishment. Interpretations may vary, but each should reveal the positive message of the Truth in some manner. This is true for Torah, Koran, and all sacred texts, not just the Bible. Human life is about learning, and dealing with negative and false influences is one of the ways we learn.

The Truth is basic, consistent, and honest, and man's interpretation of the Truth has become anything but. God's message of the Truth is completely positive. We have the ability to know the Truth, disregard the nontruths, and lead satisfying, content, and complete lives.

I am not intending to discredit the Bible. The discovery of the Gnostic Gospels in Nag Hammandi, Egypt, in 1945, as well as the discovery of the Dead Sea Scrolls, gave evidence of the existence of more writings and books. How much more is buried or lost? Why are Archives of the Vatican kept secret? Historians have begun uncovering much information. This is not to discredit, but to give understanding. We are beginning to see the Truth surface as a result, and in time, the religious practices of the world will change. I would like to encourage everyone to look into the history of the Bible and religion. What you find might amaze you and confirm what you already know to be true from within your soul.

The Life of Jesus Christ

Jesus Christ is and has been the most talked about and influential man that ever lived. His life and his death changed the world. He walked this earth teaching God's message of the Truth approximately two thousand years ago. Realizing the time he came, the short amount of time he spent teaching, and that he spoke to all people, is to recognize the simplicity of God's message of the Truth. God's message of the Truth was not meant to be complicated. Jesus taught the universal message of God's Truth to all people, and the message was meant for all mankind, not any one group. Jesus claimed no religious faith, nor did he establish a faith.

Jesus was born to a common family and lived a humble life. His disciples were common people, not religious leaders or scholars. His message was for all mankind, not just a select few or a chosen group. He turned no one away and extended love to all. He did not require a temple, lavish surroundings, or any structure as a meeting place when he was teaching. He did not require gifts, money, or donations from anyone in order for them to be a follower or to listen to his message. During the time Jesus spent on earth, he only asked that you listen, trust, and have faith in his words, the words of God, and live your life according to his teachings. Jesus lived and spoke the wisdom and love of the Truth.

The teachings and life of Jesus were about living a life of love, integrity, humility, peace, compassion, and forgiveness; to have goodwill toward all, to help those in need, and to have faith in God. Jesus taught that God, his father, is the father of all mankind (we are all one), that God loves us unconditionally, and that we are created in his image (the light of God is within our souls).

None of the teachings of Christ were negative or instructed us to be judgmental about others. He did not teach, participate in, or promote punishment, nor cause harm to anyone. He stopped the stoning of the prostitute to demonstrate to us the power of love, compassion, and forgiveness. What better example do we have of tolerance and nonjudgment? He taught that each of us has the ability to learn from our mistakes and errors. Jesus did not put up a fight when the Romans arrested him, and he told his disciples not to fight or retaliate. What he did was forgive his captors. Jesus did not promote violence, conflict, or retaliation.

Jesus taught us to forgive and love our enemies and those that cause us harm. He taught us if you cause harm to yourself or others, your life will be difficult and you will create your own punishment. His message taught us when you live according to God's message of the Truth and have faith, you become enlightened and know the joys of life, no matter what is happening in the physical world.

The only sign of discontentment Jesus displayed was his frustration over people not listening to his message. To get their attention, he started performing miracles and healing the sick. The miracles not only occurred, but were meant to be symbolic of having faith. If you have faith in God's message of love, you can heal your life. Not only could the blind man see, but this is also symbolic that faith opens the doors to your soul so you can see clearly and realize what matters in life. He cleared the merchants from the Temple to remove the worship of money and the material life, and to demonstrate the necessity of reverence for God. Reverence for God is reverence for life.

The resurrection of Christ caused him and his teachings to become immortalized. Jesus Christ's earthly death and resurrection demonstrated to us eternal life and the presence of God in our lives. The crucifixion illustrated it is faith that overcomes all obstacles, and living a life devoted to God is not about the material world. The arrest, trial, and death of Jesus were the ultimate demonstrations of the values of the Truth. He showed love, integrity, humility, and peace with his actions, and he extended compassion and forgiveness to his captors and executioners.

The crucifixion of Christ completely bewildered and frightened the disciples. They were expecting Christ the Messiah to lead them to a new kingdom of the Promised Land. This message was misunderstood. Jesus taught living the values of the Truth is the way to heal our lives, and is the path to enlightenment. The kingdom he described is not a physical place, but it is the state of being of love.

After his death, Jesus appeared to Mary Magdalene and told her to carry on his word and he would always be with her. He appeared to the disciples and Paul with the same message, instructing them to teach God's Truth to all. The resurrection of Jesus gave new meaning to life with the possibility of life after death. It is his death that we focus on because of its profound effect, but it is more important for us to focus on his life as an example of how to live our lives.

The life of Jesus was full of adversity, but this did not stop him from living the Truth. When you think about the life of Jesus and the teachings of the Bible, ask yourself these questions. Did Jesus speak of God in any way other than loving, with compassion and forgiveness to all? Did Jesus refuse to accept anyone based on their beliefs, condition, or nationality? Did Jesus cause harm to anyone or threaten anyone with punishment? Did Jesus support violence or punishment? Did Jesus preach shame, guilt, fear, resentment, or anger? The life of Jesus Christ only reflected love, kindness, and giving to all, and this was the basis for his teachings and the purpose of the stories he told. It is only man's misunderstandings and misinterpretations, due to the ego-mind, that have created any meanings that do not reflect the values of the Truth. The teachings of Jesus Christ were positive, inspirational, and meant to open the doors of our souls. His teachings were not meant to create negativity or judgment, and close the doors to our souls.

Jesus taught the importance of faith. He performed miracles to demonstrate the power of faith. Faith gives your life meaning and changes your life. The only interpretation of the Bible possible is to realize what the life of Jesus stood for, the message he taught, and how he lived his life. To know this, is to know any negatives found in the gospels or scriptures that do not align with the messages of the Truth, are the creation of man's ego, and not the word of Jesus or God.

Religion and Consciousness

Religion serves as a link to God for many, but we are divided in our beliefs. Historically, religions have been based on the conformity of the practice of rules and regulations, not on the promotion of individuality or the Truth. God's message of the Truth is not about conforming to any one religion, but is based on love, faith, and the relationship you have with him from within your soul. Becoming conscious, connected to your soul, and one with God is not dependent on being part of a religious faith.

God is not any more honored by a large, lavish service and formal place of worship, than he is by any simple prayer or conversation from any place we choose. God is available to all of us at all times, in all places, with no rules to follow or rituals to practice. God does not care how, when, or where you communicate with him. You can communicate with God anywhere, anytime, in any manner that works for you. You do not need formal or prewritten prayers; you can pray formally or informally. You can simply talk, shout, think, or sing out loud or in silence, when communicating with God. You do not need a middleman to talk to God. You can talk directly to God yourself. The power of prayer, or however you communicate, is in the faith and sincerity. God is honored by what is within your heart. When you are communicating with Jesus, any of the ascending masters, angels, or spirit guides, you are communicating with God.

Reverence for God comes from our knowing the goodness, the power, the glory, and love that is God. Reverence is not the result of feelings of fear and unworthiness. Our relationship with God is to be one of love not fear. God does not want us to grovel at his feet. He wants us to be responsible for our lives, honor ourselves and others, and live his message of the Truth.

We are all equal in God's eyes. I cannot stress this point enough. No one is any better than anyone else. We are seen as individual souls on different paths in life. We are free to make choices based on our own free will as to the direction our paths follow. It is up to us to discover and follow our path by living an authentic life and striving to fulfill our divine purpose.

Whether you are more in tune to an eastern philosophy, western philosophy, both, or no philosophy, what matters is *how* you live your life. As you advance spiritually and seek a higher level of understanding, you may choose any number of practices and these may change from time to time. Spirituality and oneness with God comes from within and is enhanced by continuing to open wide the doors of your soul.

The goal of this life is to become one with our soul and one with God. Since God is not someone we can physically see and touch, we have to rely on faith and the knowledge of the Truth that is inherent within our souls. God loves us and is there for us at all times. Becoming conscious can occur in an infinite number of ways, with no right or wrong way. We each need to come to terms with ourselves and with God in our own way. Being one with our soul and with God is right, no matter how it happens.

It is easy to lose your way in the distortions that have become part of many religious cultures. As you become conscious and more connected to your soul, your understanding of God and the Truth will increase and change. At some point, this may cause you to pull away from your religion or faith while searching for a higher meaning. Even if you pull away to search for higher meaning, you may still choose to practice your faith for reasons of service, community, structure, family, or for any reason you feel necessary. The way is up to you. The destination is the same for each of us, and we arrive in our own time and in our own way.

Becoming conscious and connected to your soul may involve religion, but religion is not necessary. Consciousness is an individual process that for many goes beyond the practice of a religious faith.

9

Spirituality

The concept of spirituality or the presence of God cannot be explained, proved, or disproved by intellect or science. Science is not able to prove or disprove the existence of the soul, since it is not a part of the physical body. Science and intellect have criteria you must be able to see, touch, and positively identify, for anything to exist. Until the criteria changes, science and intellect will continue to raise doubts, even though there has been scientific documentation of patients being medically healed as a result of prayer and faith.

God and the Universe are greater than, and out of the realm of, science and intellect. Belief must be accepted and embraced based on faith, inner knowing, and spiritual experiences. The proof lies within the souls of each of us.

Spirituality means different things to different people. Spirituality for many is their faith and belief in God. For others it is about being connected to their inner self, whether God is included in the equation or not. Spirituality is a term often overused and misunderstood. It is more than a self-image or a belief in God.

Spirituality is living a life based on the Truth by striving to become conscious and connected to your soul. It is living from within your soul by being true and honest with yourself, honoring life, striving to fulfill your life's purpose, and listening to and following the guidance of the intuition of your soul. Spirituality brings love, peace, and harmony into your life, and gives life meaning. A spiritual life is lived with the passion of fulfilling your dreams and desires. Spirituality is becoming conscious and empowering your soul. Spirituality is about living your life authentically with divine guidance. Spirituality is discovering who you really are and living your life with meaning. When you live from within your soul, you will come alive spiritually.

Spirituality embraces all religious faiths and accepts all mankind, realizing we are all one. Spirituality is a way of life, not a practice, with no rules or regulations to follow. Spirituality does not require you to sacrifice who you are, give up everything material, or sacrifice having fun. A spiritual life is lived from within your soul and in harmony with human life. A spiritual life is a life of service and not sacrifice. Service is living your best life not only for yourself, but also for the betterment of all mankind. A life of service is honoring yourself and others, and creating positive energy, no matter whether your role of service is direct or indirect.

We are naturally hungry for our connection with God. Our superficial lifestyle has left us spiritually starved, due to living our lives unconsciously, and depriving ourselves of who we are and why we are here. Many are searching for a spiritual connection and we have made it more difficult than it needs to be. We need to realize this is earth, we are humans, human life is supposed to have its up and downs, and we are here for a reason. Being spiritual will not give you special powers that will make you immune to life's events. Being spiritual will change your focus and how you live your life, which will enable you to live a full, content, and satisfied life, no matter what twists and turns, or highs and lows, you experience along the way.

Living a spiritual life in our western culture is difficult. Spirituality is not openly supported or embraced, and we really do not deal with much of anything that has to do with feelings of the inner self. Spirituality is viewed and dealt with by society in much the same way it deals with mental illness and abuse, knowing it is real but basically ignoring it exists. The superficial, materialistic life is what is real to us, it makes sense to us, and it is how we value ourselves and judge others. It is what our society accepts and supports. Being spiritual in many ways is to be out of step with society.

Religion has been a part of our culture for hundreds of years, and we understand and accept the concept of religion. Spirituality and religion are both accepted by our society, as long as they do not interfere with society's daily life and stay within our homes, churches, synagogues, temples, etc. Religious faiths have places of worship and specific books and written rules to follow, but we don't live religion as part of our daily lives. Spirituality on the other hand is a way of life.

Spirituality is not something you become or an organization you become part of. It is the journey of your life, and it is *how* you live your life from within your soul. A spiritual life is a journey, one in which you will continue to learn and grow on the path to enlightenment for your entire life. It does not mean everything will be easy or perfect. In fact, the journey is often challenging and difficult. Spirituality does not mean, "I'm spiritual, I believe, I pray, I meditate, I'm doing my part. I wonder why God is not doing his part. Why is my life not better and why do bad things keep happening? I told God he could guide my life, so why isn't he?" Just because you believe does not mean you can sit back and enjoy the ride. The journey requires you to become an active participant. You have to do the work and live the life. Living a conscious, spiritual life is a choice only you make for yourself.

Living a spiritual life is not about preaching to others, quoting the Bible, appearing as a religious scholar or leader, or trying to convert everyone to your way of thinking. You can affect the lives of others with your energy by becoming a living example of the values of the Truth. People do not need to be preached to, they just need to be inspired to seek the knowledge from within. More is gained by your actions and your energy, than by your words. For example, you can tell someone you love them a thousand times a day, but words mean nothing unless your actions demonstrate love. Try walking down the street or going shopping in a positive mood, and genuinely smile and make eye contact with those you pass by. See how a complete stranger responds to your energy and act of kindness, and notice how it can change not only their mood but your own.

Being spiritual is *how* you live your life, not what you do for a living or what faith you practice. It is *how* the values of the Truth affect your job, relationships, family, hobbies, etc. Being spiritual does not mean you have to be a scholar of theology, a devout follower of a faith, a priest, a nun, rabbi, monk, elder, etc. None of these will make you spiritual. You can be anything you want to be and you do not have to be anything other than ordinary. You can be spiritual being a mother, a father, ditch digger, teacher, doctor, candlestick maker, salesman, baker, or anything that you desire. You do not have to practice or belong to a faith, go to church, or read the Bible or other sacred texts. You may want to belong to a faith for the structure, for being part of a group, or for any reason you choose. Some have the need to be aligned with a faith, and some do not. Each of us is an individual and we need to customize our lives to fit our needs. The Truth is the only constant.

Many expect a spiritual life to be more complicated than it really is. The Truth is constant and much easier to follow than the rules of society or a religious faith. Spirituality is not about religious practices and rituals, unless you want these to be part of your life. It is not important to God whether you practice rituals or that you celebrate any of the holy days, including Christmas and Easter. God cares that you live your best life by being true to yourself, working toward fulfilling your purpose, and striving to live the values of the Truth to the best of your ability. The way is up to you.

The spiritual journey for each of us is unique, yet the destination is the same for everyone. Becoming conscious, connecting with your soul, and becoming one with God is the same experience for everyone, but it happens to each of us in our own way, and is accomplished individually. Being spiritual is not about doctrines, rituals, special techniques, certain lifestyle, or special diets. Living the Truth and communication with God are all that is necessary. The practices you choose will usually depend on your background, culture, and the influences in your life. Any practices you choose that work for you are the right practices for you.

We are born with the knowledge of the Truth within our souls. The knowing is innate within each and every one of us. Many search for the connection with God and their soul through external sources and find they are unable to connect, no matter how much they try. The connection will not come from religious practices, books, seminars, workshops, another person, etc. These are valuable sources for inspiration, validation, and enhancement, but the connection must come from within you. You do not have to develop the knowing, you already have it. You just need to open the doors to your soul by becoming conscious.

We are living in a great time of change with many wonderful spiritual teachers and sources for the message of the Truth. Keep in mind we are in human form and our egos are vulnerable to being misled. It is easy to become misguided by following rules, doctrines, and traditions. The Truth has no secrets or hidden agendas. Accept only that which aligns with the Truth and knowledge within your soul. Do not trust blindly by becoming spiritually naive or by seeing the world through rose-colored glasses.

True spiritual teachers are humble and willing to share the Truth freely with no motives of self-glorification or glamorization. Their purpose will be to convey the Truth. It is their desire to inspire others to open the door of their souls and to share the experience of the warmth, peace, love, and contentment the Truth provides. A teacher is not someone who dictates or controls the knowledge you receive or the direction you follow. A great teacher is one that inspires, stimulates, validates, and enhances your knowledge as a means to enrich your life, empower your soul, and motivate you to discover that which is within your soul.

When becoming devoted to the living the Truth, you will find your life's journey will take on a new dimension, doors will open, and your life will change more than you could ever imagine. God, Jesus Christ, the ascending masters, spirit guides, and angels are available at all times to provide divine guidance. Invite them into your life and allow them to be your teachers, guides, and inspiration. They are really the only teachers you need. When the student is ready, the teacher will appear. Surrender to God and accept the guidance that awaits within you. Living a spiritual life is living a conscious life.

Part 4

10

Consciousness

The journey of life is a process that changes as we age. We are born dependent, as teenagers we seek independence, then as adults we become involved in jobs, raising families, and trying to get through life the best way we can. As we age and mature, we begin to realize life is not what we thought it would be. At some point we realize the end will come and we do not want to see our lives as shallow, empty, and without meaning. It is usually after many twists and turns, ups and downs, that we finally say, "Wait a minute. What is this all about? There has to be a better way."

Becoming conscious will change your life to a life with meaning and living what matters. Consciousness is awaking your soul and connecting with your soul. Consciousness is the awareness and the connection to the light of God within your soul. Becoming one with God is important so divine guidance can work with you and through you. When you are connected to your soul, the inner knowing of the Truth will come to you. The knowingness of the Truth is not of your mind, but of your soul. You have to *feel it from within to know it*. You will know the Truth when it comes to you. Knowing it and feeling it is like feeling your breath when you breathe. You cannot see the air, but you feel it and know it when the air fills your lungs.

Becoming conscious is a continuous journey of an advancing relationship with your soul and with God. What will becoming conscious bring to your life? Integrity, humility, peace, compassion, and forgiveness will become part of how you live your life, as you learn the meaning of love. You will become responsible for all aspects of your life, see your experiences as ways to learn life's lesson, and accept yourself and others without judgment. The results of striving to live a conscious life are inner peace, contentment, satisfaction, and living authentically. Consciousness will create a balance between your soul, your ego, and the external world so what is going on around you will not rock your boat. You will still be affected by your ego, but you will not be caught up blindly in its wants and neediness, unless you allow it.

Consciousness is to live your life being directed by the intuition of your soul and aligning your thoughts, emotions, feelings, intentions, and actions with the values of the Truth. Consciousness gives you the wisdom and the knowledge to learn and grow from your mistakes, errors, success, and failures. Living a conscious life is living a life on a solid foundation of rock (the Truth), instead of an unconscious life lived on an unstable foundation of sand (nontruths, distortions, and illusions) that could wash away at any moment. A conscious life is lived from within your soul. An unconscious life is lived from your ego-mind.

Consciousness is like living your life with the lights on. When there is light, you are able to see clearly, and the lessons of your life will be exposed to you as you become ready to deal with them. You will realize your strengths and weakness, discover your talents and creativity, and live what really matters. The light being on in your life is a result of opening the doors of your soul.

Becoming conscious is to become an individual and gain self-esteem. This will empower you to make choices from within your soul, and not from your ego-mind or from the

influences of others and society. When you have s(
everything in your life will improve. This will include you.
physical well-being, your mental and emotional states, and
your outlook on life. You will handle life's situations differently by detaching, surrendering, and letting go, instead of being
absorbed in the effects. You will realize you are responsible for
your life, others are responsible for theirs, and situations and
experiences are neither good nor bad, just a necessary part of
life from which to learn and grow.

Becoming conscious will give you the feeling of "having
everything." As the saying goes, "When you have your health,
you have everything." When you are conscious, you will have
an inner wellness and peace, and this is "having everything."
This is the result of creating a positive energy flow in your life.
This will be true no matter what your physical condition; even
if you become seriously or terminally ill, you will simply deal
with your life differently. A wonderful example is Christopher
Reeve. He and his family show us how love is the answer, and
how love feeds the soul. His life is an inspiration and demon-
stration of how to live an authentic life for the greater good of
self and all mankind. His purpose in life is being shown not
only to the world, but in a much different manner than he or
anyone would have expected.

Becoming conscious is the discovery process. This is a
unique and individual process for each of us, since each of us
is on a different path and at a different level of consciousness.
Becoming conscious is a journey that requires faith and connecting with your soul. The process requires that you surrender
your life to God and let go of your ego and emotional attachments to the physical world that block your way. This will create an uncluttered and free environment so your soul can come
alive. You will break the barriers and cut the strings that keep
you functioning like a puppet.

As you become conscious, the conscious self will start to
take over the unconscious self. You will live your life much the

same way, still working, having hobbies, raising a family, etc., but your approach will be different. You will remove the non-truths and the unnecessary stuff that is negative or does not feed your soul. The superficial, material life will become less distracting, and your wants, needs, and desires will change. You will remove yourself from situations that lack integrity. Your lifestyle, based on the value of the Truth, will become simpler and more focused as a result.

When you become inspired to live your life consciously, the changes you make may be minor or drastic, and will more than likely improve or deteriorate your current situation. You may change jobs, marry, divorce, move, leave friendships, gain friendships, etc. You will restructure your worldly life to fit your conscious life.

Becoming conscious will maximize your potential to learn and grow, by giving your life a richness that can be realized no other way. You will come to know that true joy, pleasure, peace, and love are realized from within. Connecting with your soul enables you to discover your life's true purpose and meaning.

Consciousness is a positive state of energy. Consciousness is living with integrity as a basis for all decisions and choices, and living your life with humility, gratitude, passion, and respect for all life. Consciousness is realizing the qualities of the ego are fear, conflict, resentment, envy, shame, guilt, and the need to win and be right at all costs. It is knowing the ego is the source of negative feelings, and understanding the ego is a necessary part of life from which you learn many of life's lessons.

As you become conscious and connected to your soul, your priorities, perceptions, goals, and values will start to change. You will know when you are on the right path by the way you feel. The important aspects and experiences of your life will begin to fall into place. You will begin to see situations differently as you learn life's lessons. Something you ordinarily would see as a big deal will no longer have the same effect. You will realize when you are acting inappropriately, not being true to yourself, or causing harm to yourself and others. You will realize the difference of how you feel when your actions and thoughts are based on love, integrity, humility, peace, compassion, and forgiveness, and when they are not.

Being conscious is a lifestyle, not a happening or an event. It is not an exclusive organization available to only a chosen few, and it is not dependent on religion, nationality, or culture. The ability to become conscious and connect with your soul is available to all mankind, and each of us is born with the natural ability and the natural desire. Becoming aware and connected is an individual process that each of us must discover for ourselves. No one can perform a ritual that will transform your life to this state. Exterior sources have the ability to inspire you to connect with your soul, enhance your awareness, and validate what you feel and know. But, the true motivation and desire to become conscious must come from within your soul. Exterior sources cannot give you the knowingness you already have within your soul or connect you with it. Inspiration will open the door, but you must walk through the door on your own.

Ultimately, you are the only one who develops any aspect of your being. You have to do the work. You cannot be a proficient or great musician, athlete, partner, friend, parent, employee, leader, conscious individual, etc., unless you make the effort and continue the effort. Awareness, knowledge, and even skill alone will not produce results. Just like any skill or talent, you must continue to learn, practice, and perform to stay at the top of your game. You cannot lose weight and keep if off, or stop an addiction, without having the desire and commitment to do the work, change your lifestyle, and continue the discipline. Consciousness is a continuous process. Know that you never stop growing in consciousness, and there is no finish line to cross. It will become easier and second nature, but it will take constant effort, desire, and commitment. Do not look for an ending, but embrace the journey.

Living a conscious life is difficult in the world today due to social environment and materialistic values. It is difficult to live a conscious life when having it all is based on the material world's desires. The priorities of a conscious life do not always align with the priorities of the material world. Not that goals and successes in the material world are not important, but it is the manner in which you attain these, and where your focus lies, that makes the difference. Today's lifestyle leaves little time for one's self. To become conscious and balance it all, you will need to spend time with you.

Becoming conscious has the appearance of being complicated and difficult to achieve, due to the many roadblocks created by the ego-mind and our lifestyle. Some of the greatest barriers are the fears and doubts created by your ego's insecurities, the expectations of others, influences from society, and the many stigmas associated with religious beliefs. Over time, when you perform in life rather than live your life from within, you will feel shallow, and you will more than likely become frustrated and dissatisfied with life. True satisfaction, contentment, and passion in life comes from developing your talents as a result of living life from within your soul. You will not tackle becoming conscious until you have the desire to discover who you really are and what your life is really about.

Many feel they are conscious and have the outward appearance of being conscious, because they believe in God or are religious. Believing in God and/or being religious are often confused with being conscious and connected to the soul. Being conscious is living life from within your soul, and living the values of the Truth. It is not what you know or what you believe in, but rather what you do with what you know or believe in, that is important. It is *how* you live your life.

Many do not achieve consciousness simply because they are not aware of the necessity to go within, have not given themselves permission to do so, or feel they are not worthy. We have been conditioned to believe connecting is a process that occurs outside of our being, or is the result of practicing a faith. Looking to external sources, such as, going to church, becoming a member of a faith, reading the sacred texts, attending workshops and seminars, will not give you consciousness or make you conscious. All of these do have the ability to inspire, enhance, and validate your inner knowing, and are great sources of support and inspiration, but it is the realization from within that makes the difference. When you feel inspired, you are opening doors to our soul, so you can feel the knowing and make the connection to God.

Becoming conscious is like catching the ball and running with it. There will be those who will help you on your path and those who will create interference. The challenge is to stay balanced and focused. It is not easy, just know it is the ego-mind that creates the illusion and makes it seem more difficult than it needs to be. Consciousness is not like walking a tightrope where you are constantly struggling not to fall. Falling is part of learning life's lessons. Life is about learning and growth, and not about being easy or trying to be perfect.

The journey is challenging, but at the same time it is the most wonderful experience of your life. God and the Universe are waiting to welcome you and will be there for you, but they will not chase after you. The desire must come from within you. Realize consciousness has no exact paths or rules to follow. Your path is between God and you. Customize your path to fit your needs and beliefs, not the needs or beliefs of anyone else. If you make the choice to follow your spiritual path, and connect with your soul, the rewards will absolutely amaze you.

When you are conscious and connected to your soul, you will no longer excuse your behavior or blame it on someone else. You will deal with, and focus on, the *causes* in your life's experiences, instead of living unconsciously in the effects. Will you still get angry, upset, hurt, and judge others? Yes, but the effect will be different. The difference will be that you will catch yourself. You will begin to deal with situations by seeking understanding and learning from the experience. You will detach and see the situation more clearly. You will know no matter what happens, all things happen for a reason, and the results are as they should be so you can learn.

Consciousness is like gaining sight when you have been in the darkness. Consciousness allows you to be receptive to the messages that will guide you on the journey of your life. You never know when the inspiration to become conscious will occur, or where it will come from. When you are open to receiving messages and are accepting of your life, you will receive the inspiration. When you are ready, the teacher will appear. It may be something as simple as a comment that gets your attention, and suddenly your life's direction is changed in an instant. Many times the reality of consciousness is realized due to a spiritual experience, and in some cases, the reality of a spiritual experience does not have an impact on your life until a much later time.

It is easy to get caught up in the expectations of what you think a conscious life should be, and inhibit it from happening. You cannot force becoming conscious. You will need to listen and feel the whispers of the knowing from within your soul. You will need to relax and let the process flow. If you struggle to make it happen, your ego will be involved, and you will only become frustrated and create negative energy. Becoming conscious will take courage because it will change your life.

Being conscious does not mean nirvana or that you will blissfully sail off into the sunset for the rest of your life. Know the road will be smooth at times, difficult at others. When times are difficult, the road will be full of potholes, bumps, and washed out areas, but the road will be smooth if you choose to see it that way. You will deal with life differently. You will see situations and experiences as part of the learning process. You will have the contentment of inner peace and develop an underlying positive attitude, knowing no matter what occurs, it happened for a reason. You will realize human life is perfect as it is, and satisfaction in life comes from within. The fear of becoming conscious is created by the ego-mind. The soul gives only clear answers. The ego-mind is the source of false and misleading answers and doubts. The ego-mind is concerned with what if, why, what will they think, the past, the future, and superficial matters. We are used to the workings of our ego-minds and unfamiliar with the workings of our souls. Herein lies the challenge and the struggle. Know nothing the ego-mind can dish out, will distract you, unless you allow it.

To meet the challenge, you will need to release the negativity and resentments from the painful events of your life. It is a process that will cause you to peel away the layers of your emotions and feelings. Just when you think you have dealt with a major issue or fear, you will continue to find more issues to deal with. One thing will seem to lead to another, but this is how progress is made. As you start to connect with your soul and work at peeling away the many layers of your emotions and feelings, you will feel freer and more at peace. You will gain a clearer understanding of the values of the Truth and their relationship to the *causes* of your emotions and feelings.

When you are conscious, you will become responsible for everything that happens in your life. Even when you accept responsibility for all that happens, there will still be situations you will not understand. Do not dwell on or internalize experiences you do not understand, or punish yourself, no matter what has happened. This will only create negative energy. Instead, go within, seek understanding, view the situation from the values of the Truth, allow yourself time to learn and to move on with wisdom. When you do not understand, ask for guidance, release what you do not understand, and move on. Know you will not understand every experience, but generally, you will come to over time.

Detaching, surrendering, and letting go are necessary to release your doubts and fears and break free from the comfort zone of an ego-based life. To do this, you must be willing to be honest with yourself. When you are honest with yourself about how you feel, you will gain understanding and acceptance, and have the ability to silence your ego-mind.

Living a conscious life is impossible to maintain one hundred percent of the time. The ego will always be a part of your earthly existence, and you will slip back into your ego's way of thinking as part of the process. However, once you connect with your soul, the reality of the Truth will keep pulling you toward consciousness. A conscious life will give you a sense of contentment that will encompass you and enable you to live your life authentically. When you are ready to take on the challenge, you will know it, even though there may be many false starts before you become truly committed. Do not wait or hold back, thinking there has to be a specific moment or event that will make the change for you. Many times it is the smallest, most insignificant moment that creates the greatest change.

When you are conscious, your life will be about feeding your soul. You will know when you are in the right job or relationship and when you are moving in the right direction, and you will be free to make changes. You will realize the choices you make may not give you the results you were expecting, but they will be the results you need to continue shaping your life's journey. Being conscious is realizing change is a constant part of life. One thing leads to another. When one door closes, being conscious will allow the next appropriate door to open. Being conscious will allow you to be guided by the intuition of your soul. Listen and pay attention to what you feel from within, and have patience so you can learn.

Living an unconscious life is like graduating from high school and not being able to read. When you are not conscious of your soul, and there will be an emptiness deep inside that you will try to fill. Filling the void can take on many faces. You may try to fill the void by getting lost in the addictions of food, drugs, alcohol, spending, working, or simply in the melodramas of life. You may seek power and control, look to material achievements for fulfillment, or turn to any other distraction that fits your needs. Becoming conscious will fill the voids and emptiness in your life, but the choice is up to you.

Life is never about just one event. Do you feel like your life is on hold, waiting for an event, something, or anything to change, so your life will become what you want it to be? Are you waiting to find your soul mate, the right job, or when . . . happens I will be able to . . .? Do you feel you are covered with so many layers of stuff, expectations, and burdens that if someone would just give you that 'something' to fix your life, everything would be wonderful? Or, at some point, do you realize what you have been waiting for only satisfied you temporarily, not at all, or did not change your life the way you thought it would?

We want life to be easy. Everyone wants the fairy tale, so they can live happily ever after. We seem to have this fantasy it can happen, if only . . . . Somehow, we still think an easy life is a rite of passage. Waiting for this 'something' to happen only causes frustration. You have to accept the process at face value by dealing with issues as they arise, and having faith in the journey by continuing to learn and grow. As you learn, grow, and follow the intuition of your soul, the challenges and struggles will decrease. This will be the result of changing your perception and attitude. Live your life now, this moment, not some day when.

Being conscious is living now, in the present moment. Living in the present moment will keep you in a positive state of energy, realizing at any given moment you have no problems, and only past and future thoughts create problems and negative energy. When you live in the present moment, you will look forward to each day of your life without living in the past or worrying about the future. Don't wait for tomorrow to start your life, tomorrow may never come. There is no time like the present moment to take charge of your life and live consciously.

Even when you are conscious, there will still be difficult times, and you will continue to stumble while finding your way. The journey of life has no shortcuts. You have to learn to walk before you can run, and you will usually fall many times in the process. There will be times of great clarity and times of great despair. It is easy to get lost in being human. Just know this is part of the process. You will go along being humble, peaceful, loving, compassionate, and forgiving, only to find yourself being angry, depressed, judgmental, jealous, resentful, rude, selfish, greedy, etc. When you are connected to your soul and this occurs, you will be aware of what is happening and what you are doing or have done, and you will know you are responsible for your actions, choices, and intentions. You will no longer claim innocence or place blame elsewhere. You will know in some way you have created the circumstances that surround you. When this occurs, you will realize you have issues to deal with and lessons to learn. Allow yourself to feel how you feel, no matter how positive or negative the feelings are. When you can feel your feelings, you can deal them and discover their cause.

Becoming conscious will create numerous changes in your life. Those in your inner circle may not like or accept your changes. Your job may no longer satisfy your inner creativity and passion. At times, the journey may even leave you feeling lonely. There will be times when you will feel like you are being tested. Realize this is you testing yourself as a result of your ego-mind creating doubt. Sometimes what feels like a test, is actually part of the lessons you are here to learn.

The desire to become conscious does not usually occur until you start to question life, or feel empty inside, or an event occurs that is either miraculous or tragic. It is up to you to decide at each crossroad, if the price of change is worth the

price of your growth. You can choose to ignore the inner call-
ing, continue on with your life just as it is, or begin connecting.
When you are ready to handle the journey, you will feel the
whispers from within your soul. You will experience times of
denial, and resist, pull back, and/or even stop for a while. Just
know this is part of the process. Everyone becomes conscious
individually, in their own time, and in their own way. No matter how you proceed, the awareness will always be at the core
of you, waiting until you are ready. You have the gift of free
will, so it is up to you to choose how to live your life. You can
choose to open the doors of your soul or you can choose to
leave them closed.

Becoming conscious usually takes the accumulation of
life's experiences, wake-up calls and hitting bottom to be humble enough to start the journey. When you are ready, you will
go within for the answers. Ask God and the Universe for help
and be sincere in your requests. Be patient. The answers will
not always be what you want, be what you expect, or be there
when you want them. You will not always get what you ask for,
but you will get what you need to help you learn and grow. Just
know that everything happens for a reason, and things happen
as they are supposed to, so you can learn. Once you accept this
and trust it, you will no longer say, "Why me!" or "Why is this
happening when I have been working so hard at focusing on
being conscious?" Most of the time there is not a direct cause
and effect that makes sense to us on the surface. This is because
we search for the meaning from our ego-mind's point of view,
not from within our soul.

Becoming conscious is a challenge, but we make it much
more complicated then it needs to be. The Truth is simple, pure,
basic, consistent, and timeless. We search outside of ourselves
for some startling revelation when everything we need is within our souls. We have been given the compass within our souls
to find our way. We are given hints and signs along the way, but
we must be willing to recognize them. God sent the ascending

masters to teach us the message of the Truth. They taught the Truth and lived the Truth. They are the best examples for how to live our lives. God loves us and wants the best for us. It is up to us to realize it.

Becoming conscious is realizing nothing in the material world matters, human life is an illusion, and the growth of the soul is the purpose of human life. Once you accept you are responsible for your thoughts, emotions, feelings, choices, and intentions, the meaning of your life will change. When you realize you can no longer blame anyone or anything for what happens, your life will change. When you accept you were born at the right time and to the family, and there are no accidents, coincidences, unscheduled events, or victims, and that life is fair, your life will change. All of this may be a lot to accept, but acceptance creates learning and growth.

Consciousness is being in touch with who you are so you can learn life's lessons and advance toward enlightenment. The success of your life's journey is up to you. You can choose to make consciousness the focus of your life, deal with it on a part-time basis, or even not at all. It is easy to become busy living the materialistic life and hard to take the time for a conscious life. Living a conscious life in our society is not the norm. Choosing to focus on your life's journey will mean breaking free from the norm and making time to become a conscious individual.

You are the only one who can change your life. No one else can change your life for you, and you cannot make anyone else change. Happenings, circumstances, and others may inspire you to change, but you are the one who makes your own changes. Change requires desire, courage, commitment, and determination. The journey will not always be easy, and it is not supposed to be. Once you make the choice there will be no turning back. You will still have doubts and struggles, waver back and forth at times, even stop for a while, but you will continue to be drawn on your path.

A conscious journey is not easy, but neither is an unconscious journey. When you are conscious, there will be times of frustration and doubt, but once you feel the connection you will be drawn to it. You will realize it is the only time when you feel true inner peace and contentment in your life. Being conscious is not about an easy life. It is about learning and growth. Being conscious is the ability to learn, and you learn because you are conscious. When you make living the values of the Truth the focus of your life, you will incorporate them into your thoughts, choices, intentions, and actions. There are thousands of ways to travel the journey of a conscious life. Becoming conscious and living the Truth are how, but the way is up to you.

11

Self-Esteem, Honoring Yourself

Honoring yourself is having self-esteem. Self-esteem does not exist without an inner connection to the love from within your soul. Self-esteem is discovered and realized by becoming conscious and connecting with your soul. Honoring yourself with self-esteem creates positive energy. Self-esteem allows you to be who you are and move in the direction of your life's purpose.

When you have self-esteem, you become an individual. Each of us is unique and special in our own way, from the way we look, to our DNA, and our fingerprints. We were meant to be individuals. Becoming an individual allows you the freedom to connect with your soul, so your soul can become your identity. Becoming an individual removes labels that prohibit you from being who you truly are. Removing labels allows you to express your creativity, talents, and desires from within your soul. When you are connected to your soul, you will realize your own uniqueness and your similarities to all mankind.

Being an individual with self-esteem is not common in our society, or in the world for that matter. Why don't more of us have self-esteem? Most individuals do not develope true self-esteem because it is often repressed. Rulers, governments, and religions, seeking power and control, have suppressed self-esteem for many hundreds of years. The concept of self-esteem has started to surface, since many are asking, "Who am I and why am I here?" Self-esteem is talked about, many books written on the topic, and it is the topic of discussion on many talk shows. We are aware of its important, but we are not sure what it is or how to get it.

In realizing what self-esteem is, we realize what it is not. The illusion of self-esteem is seen as vanity, pride, power, control, superiority, status, and/or the success of having financial wealth. Self-esteem is not about superficial successes, conceit, self-absorption, self-gratification, or satisfying the wants and needs of the ego. Self-esteem is not depending on what others think about you, pleasing others, or sacrificing any part of you to become someone others think you should be. The illusions of self-esteem are the insecurities of the ego. Self-esteem is how you value who you are on the inside, and it has nothing to do with what your rank or status is, or whether you are rich or poor.

Self-esteem is when you love, accept, approve, respect, and honor yourself with self-confidence, integrity, humility, compassion, and forgiveness. Self-esteem is believing in yourself and being honest and true to yourself. Self-esteem is about being centered, and developing a relationship with yourself by being your own best friend, advisor, and confidant. When you lack self-esteem, you become your own worst enemy by not being honest and true to yourself, which creates negative energy.

Self-esteem is living with integrity and being true to your ideals and values. This results in personal happiness, inner peace, contentment, and satisfaction. It is the desire to strive to satisfy your life, at whatever level you desire, by living up to your own expectations without having to prove anything to anyone. It gives you the ability to live your life with passion and to fulfill your dreams.

Self-esteem allows you to learn from your successes, failures, mistakes, and errors without punishing yourself. Self-esteem gives you confidence to live *your life* and become creative, and the courage to take the risks necessary to become who you really are. Self-esteem is key to letting go of your ego and surrendering so you can learn life's lessons.

Self-esteem is having respect for yourself and others. Respect is not about entitlement, the result of power and control, or something you command from others. Respect is how you treat yourself and others. Respect is clearly defined by the Golden Rule. Self-esteem is self-love and love for all mankind and all creation. Self-esteem is the inner peace of embracing life.

Self-esteem is not something you acquire or accomplish. It is not an all-or-none quality, and even having a small amount is worth more than you might think. Self-esteem is a continuous learning process throughout your life. You must work at it by maintaining it and enhancing it. It is like keeping your house clean. Once you clean it, it does not permanently stay clean forever. To maintain and enhance your self-esteem, you will need update it by replacing old thoughts and feelings, with new thoughts and feelings.

No one can give you self-esteem. You can read about it, others can tell you how wonderful you are, you can win awards and achieve successes, and still not have self–esteem. The desire for self-esteem and self-worth come from within. When you are conscious, centered, and focused on being true to yourself, you will develop self-esteem.

Many are searching for approval and validation externally, from others. Approval and validation can only come from within you. Do not look to anyone other than yourself for approval. Do not make choices based on anyone else's opinions, wishes, hopes, or dreams. Listen to others for inspiration, but answer only to you. You are the only one who can approve of your life, and you are the only one who can truly disapprove of your life when you are being true to yourself. You are the only one who walks in your shoes. Self-approval has nothing to do with ego or conceit. When you approve of yourself, others will approve of you as well. This does not mean you will not meet with disapproval. There will always be someone who is envious, jealous, or just plain unhappy with their life, and will try to project their energy on to you and others.

When you do not have self-esteem, it is easy for others to project their negative energy on to you, and you will feel like a victim and blame others for your problems. Absorbing negative energy from others is not about fault or blame. Many times absorbing negative energy is a result of learned behavior. If you had parents who did not know how to express love, chances are it was the same way they grew up, and their parents before them and so on. It is up to you to break the cycle.

Gaining self-esteem takes courage and desire. The best way to acquire self-esteem is to recognize you do not have it and you want it. This usually occurs when you discover your life is not working, when you are trying to be what someone else expects you to be, when you find that you are missing 'you' in your life, and/or when you hit bottom. You must be willing to be responsible for everything that has happened in your life, both past and present, and to be honest and in touch with your thoughts, emotions, and feelings. Being in touch will result in becoming humble.

The process of gaining and maintaining self-esteem is a process that will continue your entire life. Accept, approve, and respect yourself as you are at this moment, no matter what you want to change or what you do not like about yourself. Self-esteem means facing your positive and negative qualities, your strengths and weaknesses. Self-esteem is realizing your ego is part of your life. It is dealing with who you are and not who you think you should be. This means to no longer judge, devalue, or punish yourself, and to realize that self-doubt is just an obstacle. Accepting and approving of yourself will go a long way toward removing the negative energy you associate with any part of your life. Gaining self-esteem will give you the freedom to make the changes you desire throughout your life. When you love and accept yourself, you will become the source of your well-being.

A good place to start is with your internal dialogue. These are the words you use to describe yourself and they create your self-image. Redesign your internal dialogue by referring to yourself with positive words and statements so you may create positive thoughts, feelings, and energy. Create a positive image that is realistic for where you are *now* in your life. Create this image based on what you already accept about yourself, even if it is only one thing. Create a friendship with the parts of you that you do not like, so you can create positive energy. If you are making changes in your life, refer to them as if they have already occurred, so you create the image you desire in your subconscious mind. Start your description of yourself with I am (positive terms), and not I was or I will be. Love yourself as you are now, no matter what, and continue to love yourself as your life changes. Strive to create a positive environment for yourself, at all times, so you can live consciously in the present moment.

Accepting yourself is being responsible for your life and being honest with yourself. When you are honest with yourself, you will be true to yourself, and you will trust yourself. When you are responsible for your life, you will be objective about yourself without self-blame or punishment. This will allow you to become vulnerable so you can get in touch with your thoughts, emotions, and feelings. Even when you have self-esteem, it will be hard to ignore the influences of others. Situations will still bother and upset you, but you will change how you respond, even if not initially. Being responsible for your life is realizing you create your own reality, and you have the free will to create the life you desire.

Honesty and truth are always positive energies, but we have managed to change honesty and truth into negative ener-

gy. We live in a society and world where honesty and truthfulness are hard to find. People are not honest with each other or
themselves, and being honest often results in conflicts. When
we are honest with someone, even when the intent was not
meant to be harmful or disrespectful, it often appears that way
and others become offended. As a result, we have developed a
habit of telling people what they want to hear, and we do the
same with ourselves. The reason honesty and truthfulness hurts
is because the ego is fragile, and it is the ego that is feeling hurt,
not the soul.

Being completely honest with yourself is accepting all you
feel, whether you like it or not. When you are honest with yourself and it hurts, it is because you have hit an emotional nerve
or touched on an emotional wound. When you are responsible
and honest, you will realize you need to deal with whatever the
issue is, and not dealing with it will only perpetuate the cycle.

When you are honest with yourself, it is like turning on a
light in your life. It gives you the self-confidence and the freedom to trust your intuition. Trust in the intuition of your soul
and divine guidance from God completely. Put into trust with
others only that which you are willing to be responsible for.

When you trust yourself and your intuition, you will not be
concerned with trusting others. Trust is about you and what you
will accept in your life. Learn to trust yourself completely, but
be guarded when trusting others. You will need to decide when
you can trust someone and when you cannot. If you do decide
to trust someone, do not be blind or naive. Know you are
responsible for what you decide to trust them with. When you
are connected to your soul, you will realize others will only
take from you that which you allow. You will trust others by
being responsible for what you trust them with. Only trust others with what you are willing to give away. If you do not, do
not be surprised when someone betrays your trust. If someone
does betray you, do not blame them for what you gave away.
Others will only take from you that which you allow.

Honesty and self-esteem is having humility and integrity. It is honoring your thoughts, commitments, and values with respect, love, compassion, and forgiveness. Humility is the ability to be compassionate and forgiving, and to understand, accept, and respect others, yet not compromise who you are. The reality of living a life of integrity can be difficult once you have tapped the knowledge within your soul. The reality of the awareness can be overwhelming.

When your life is about being in touch with your soul, your relationships will change. When you are striving to gain self-esteem, do not let your current relationships stop you. As you gain self-esteem, those around you will be affected. There will be those who will embrace you, and others who will resist your changing. You will begin to notice those who do not treat you or themselves with love and respect, and those you cannot be honest with. Many of these relationships will fall by the way-side. Do not look negatively at others who no longer fit into your life. Respect them for who they are and accept them as they are.

As you gain self-esteem, the environment you live in will change. You will reduce the amount of conflicts and problems in your life. Most conflicts and problems will have no place to start, since having self-esteem will silence your ego when it surfaces. When problems do arise, you will handle them more easily.

Having self-esteem as part of your being, is no easy task. Realize self-doubt will still occur. You will still be insecure at times, and even slip back into your old ways occasionally. It can even be uncomfortable in the beginning when you start dealing with your emotions and feelings. It is a task that requires time, desire, determination, commitment, and discipline. It will be almost impossible unless you take the time to take stock of your life.

Self-esteem opens doors to your soul and feeds your soul. Self-esteem is living your best life for yourself, all mankind, and creation. Self-esteem allows you to find a balance between your nonphysical life and your physical life by living the values of the Truth. Self-esteem is celebrating who you are, embracing the gift of life, and living your life authentically.

Self-esteem can only come from within your soul, and is essential to learning life's lessons. Most seek validation, love, and approval from the outside world. The outside world will only reflect back that which you are. Life is a mirror, and like attracts like. You experience in life only that which you are on the inside. When you realize this, the world will become your teacher. What you give out, you get back. Living to give, not to get, is the key. When you give freely with no expectations, you will get back what you gave and so much more.

12

Detachment

Detachment is a way to view life's experiences so you can learn life's lessons as life happens. Detachment is viewing life's experiences with love, compassion, and forgiveness. Detachment provides clarity, understanding, and acceptance, allows you to let go and surrender, and become aware of the *causes* of your experiences. Detachment is viewing life's experiences from your soul. Detachment is important in any situation, whether it is positive or negative, since valuable lessons are learned from both.

Detachment is not to be confused with being passive or in denial. Detachment is taking a step back and reflecting on a situation by removing yourself emotionally to gain clarity. Detachment is becoming an observer so you can participate in life at your highest level. You will also observe how others create their own problems, and learning occurs when you apply this to your own life. Being a detached observer allows you to learn, not only from your own experiences, but from the experiences of others.

To understand detachment is to understand attachment. Attachment is like wearing blinders or having tunnel vision. This is when you are only concerned with how the situation affects you, from your ego's point of view, and you are emotionally involved. When you are attached, you become caught up in the emotions and the effects. When you are attached to a situation, many times you will try to control the situation, or the outcome, based on the desires of your ego.

Detachment is removing your blinders so you can see clearly the circumstances that surround you. Detachment allows you to separate yourself from the emotions and become responsible for your thoughts, emotions, feelings, intentions, and actions. Detachment is to learn patience and deal with any situation peacefully and calmly. Detachment allows you to work through the situation by feeling your emotions, independently of the situation, and to participate in life without being blinded by your emotions. When you are detached from the emotions, you will ask yourself what is really going on, and you will be on your way to learning the cause. When you can relate to the cause, you can embrace and/or change your thoughts, emotions, and feelings. Detachment will contribute positive energy to any situation.

Detachment is a way of evaluating your life and becoming aware of the thoughts you have and the choices you make. Detaching from a situation allows you to see the situation as it applies to living the values of the Truth. When you are aware and conscious of your thoughts and choices, you will have the ability to make changes in your life. You will live in the world by becoming an observer with a new understanding. Detachment is a way of creating an environment to allow the message of the experience to come through, so you will make choices based on the values of the Truth, rather than the emotions of your ego. Detachment is living in the present moment.

Detachment enriches and empowers your life. Detachment allows you to learn not only from the negative experiences, but the positive as well, by not becoming caught up in either. You will no longer label and stigmatize an event or experience as a failure or success, good or bad, right or wrong. You will see experiences as opportunities to learn and grow. The purpose of detachment is to discover the *cause* of the situation by not becoming involved with the *effect*.

Your fears and your ego will prohibit you from being able to detach. The ego has no desire to detach from anything, since the ego loves the intrigue and involvement. Learning to detach takes practice, and even then there will be times when you will still react in your old familiar way. When you are in a situation and you realize your ego is surfacing, stop and pull back mentally as much as possible. Defuse the situation by breathing deeply and slowly, strive to become calm and focused, or remove yourself physically by just walking away. Realize you will not always handle every situation well. At these times, once you are removed, take a few moments to relax, detach, and view the situation. Learn as much as you can by asking yourself what is really going on. If you are like most of us, you may reflect a lot on the situation after the fact, but this is how we learn.

Learn to detach from a situation anytime an emotion is triggered that is based on your fears, neediness, and/or insecurities. The best time to detach and reflect is when you can be alone and quiet. Take time for yourself and ask yourself these questions. "What really happened?" "What was really going on?" "What am I feeling?" "What am I supposed to learn?" "What was the cause?" All the answers you need are within your soul. Be patient and kind with yourself, have faith, and ask for guidance. Let go and the answers will come to you, sometimes quickly and sometimes more slowly. In some cases, it can take years to be ready to deal with some of your emotions and feelings, but once you learn to detach and let go you will be amazed at how your life unfolds.

When you are able to detach, you will realize and accept all things happen for a reason, events are not random, and you are not in control. Detachment will give you the faith and trust that all things work out as they should. Life is a variety of constant experiences that are meant to teach us the values of the

Truth. It is not easy, but learning life's lessons is about handling life's experiences with love, peace, integrity, humility, compassion, and forgiveness. Taking a step back, separating from the experience, and focusing on the values of the Truth will help in all situations.

Detachment also allows you to step back and see the humor in life. This will become evident to you once you have been practicing detachment for a while. You will begin to see how each of us is responsible for our problems and conflicts. As a detached observer you will begin to see how many of us create the issues in our lives and how many of us thrive on playing the victim, creating drama, and keeping the pot stirred. It can be like watching an episode of "I Love Lucy," or any other comedy that resembles human life. When you are able to detach and laugh at yourself, you will have made great progress.

In *all* cases, learning life's lessons is about one or more of the values of the Truth. Learning just one can take an entire lifetime, but realize they are all interconnected. Maybe you are here to learn forgiveness, but you will not learn forgiveness without learning love, integrity, humility, peace, and compassion as part of the process. The soul sees all experiences as insight into the lesson you agreed to learn during this lifetime. Detachment is letting go and surrendering so you can learn.

13

Living in the Present Moment

Living in the present moment is the freedom to live the Truth. This is seeing your life clearly and knowing the past and the future are not relevant. Living in the present moment is the ability to detach and deal with your thoughts and emotions, and not live by reacting to them or being a victim of their effects. This is the ability to deal with change and make changes in your life. Learning and growth occurs when you live in the present moment.

When you are not living in the present moment, you are living in the memory of the past or the dream of the future. Your ego will be running your life and affecting your energy. Your focus will be on dealing with the effects of your life, and not on dealing with the causes of your thoughts, emotions, and feelings. Living in the past or the future will pull you off the course of your life's path. This is when life becomes complicated and frustrating.

It is difficult to live in the present moment when you have not dealt with past experiences that have had an adverse effect on your life. Not dealing is saying, "I am this way or my life is this way because . . . happened to me." Dealing is being responsible for your life, facing your life, and realizing your experiences are a significant part of learning the lessons in life you came here to learn. When you are responsible for your life, you will focus on living your best life, and your best life will follow. This is being in the flow of life instead of just going through the motions.

Life is a chain of events, each one affecting the other. The past is gone and if you have not learned from it, it will continue to repeat itself. The past is only relevant when you have not learned from your experiences. The future is an unknown, and you create your future with how you are living now due to your energy. Therefore, if you are living in the past, the future you create will resemble your past. Living in the present is realizing you are affecting your future with how you are living now.

When you live in the present moment, you will deal with reminders of the past as they occur. When something occurs that triggers a past memory, you will know you need to stop and take the time to detach, understand your feelings, and accept your feelings. Living in the present moment is realizing the past is to be learned from, and is not a part of your life to fall back into or be trapped in.

Living in the present moment will make your life easier, since you will not be complicating your life with baggage. When the past or negative experiences related to your karma surface, you will realize you need to deal with them and learn. When experiences are positive, you will learn from them by embracing them with gratitude. As you learn from life's experiences, you will look back at the past and be grateful for both the good and bad experiences.

When you live in the past or future, you allow your ego to surface and create stories in your mind. You will ignore your true self, become a victim of yourself, and not handle life as it happens. The ego inhibits you from living in the present moment, creates fears, and manipulates your life. The present moment does not exist where the ego is concerned, in reality, it is the past and the future that do not exist.

The only part of your life you can deal with is now, and

you shape your future with your present thoughts. Living in the present moment does not mean you will not have issues to deal with, but you will handle them as they occur and release any negative energy so you will not harbor it. The only way to deal with the past or the future is to learn by striving to live the values of the Truth. Being able to detach, accept, understand, let go, and surrender is being able to learn.

Your past becomes your future when you do not deal with your life. If you want a different future, learn from the past so you can change your life now. This does not mean you will not set goals or have dreams. It is creating a thought of the future, embracing it, feeling it, and then releasing it. Think of your desires now, as if they are happening now. Living in the present moment with goals of the future is allowing your life to unfold by not trying to control it or force it. It is trusting the outcome will be as it should be as part of your journey.

Think of your future as planting seeds in the garden of your life, and dealing with the past as weeding your garden. The future is planting thoughts (seeds) in your subconscious that will become (grow) your future. The results (amount of growth) will be reflected in the energy of your intentions. If you plant seeds that grow thorns (negative energy), you will get thorns. If you plant seeds that grow flowers (positive energy), you will get flowers. Thorns do not grow from flower seeds, and flowers do not grow from thorn seeds.

Living in the present moment is to realize there is a cause and effect for every moment in your life, and you need to deal with life as it happens. This is the reality of knowing how drastically your life can change in a moment, not knowing what the next moment will bring. Being conscious is living in the present moment. It is being aware of your soul and energy, and the ability to avoid most unwanted situations by stopping them before they start, or handling them as they happen. When you live in the present moment, you will recognize and embrace the intuition of your soul and the divine guidance you receive.

Living in the present moment is realizing you are not in control, change is going to occur whether you want it to or not, and it is the moments of your life that have the greatest impact. The gift of free will allows you to choose to live in the present moment, choose to change your thoughts, and choose to create your future. The past is part of your life's education. Review the past only to learn life's lessons and make the necessary changes.

Living in the present moment is being conscious of your thoughts, emotions, and feelings. This is accepting life and all that is, even if you do not understand it. The soul understands living in the present moment, just as the soul understands the *cause* of an experience as it is related to learning the values of the Truth.

When you are living in the present moment, you are not forcing your life to happen. You realize all of your past experiences were necessary for you to reach this point in your life, and in this reality learning occurs. You will move forward in your life, no longer carrying the baggage of the past, being guided by following your intuition and divine guidance.

The reality of living in the present moment is to know true happiness and freedom. The past is gone and the future has not happened. It is healthy to set goals and have dreams about the future, but to base your life on future dreams happening the way you want them to, is not allowing your life to flow. You can create your future, but you cannot control it.

Animals living in nature are an example of how to live in the present moment. Animals do not live in fear, worrying about the past or anticipating the future. They allow their natural instincts and learned behavior to guide them completely. They can be relaxed one minute, react to danger the next, and then go back to relaxing once the danger has passed. They deal with events and issues as they arise and then continue on. We do not realize this because we are exposed to domesticated and caged animals that no longer act as they would in nature.

Living in the present moment is to think of life as a maze. The path has many twists and turns, you know where you have been, but it is impossible to find your way back. So, you keep moving forward, not knowing what is in front of you. You can choose how you approach the maze of life. The approach can be with joy and positive intentions, by embracing all that happens, following the intuitions of your soul, or proceeding with worry, fear, and no real sense of direction. Another way to think of living in the present moment is when there is an emergency in your life. This is a time when everything stops and you are faced with what really matters. When you are forced to stop, your priorities change. You focus on what matters, and things either fall into place or you leave them behind.

Living in the present moment is living what matters. Living the values of the Truth is what matters. When you concentrate on the present moment and the values of the Truth, you will experience inner peace, contentment, and satisfaction, no matter what else is happening around you. Live your life now, knowing it is whole, perfect, and as it should be at any given moment. This allows the future to unfold and gives your life meaning. Live your life as if you have everything you need and want now, at this moment.

When you live in the present moment, you become focused on what matters in life. When you are not focused, you become distracted and achieve less satisfaction in life. Living in the present moment is embracing your life, fulfilling your desires and passions, and being conscious and connected to your soul. Realize the past is over, and tomorrow is yet a dream. The moments of our lives are what we live, and the moments teach us our greatest lessons. Think of the moments of your life as breaths of air. Ask yourself, how many breaths can you miss before life, as you know it, is gone? Then ask yourself what really matters.

14

Life Is Fair

Human life is not always easy; it can be difficult and even appear to be cruel at times, but it is always absolutely, positively fair at all times. It just does not appear that way on the surface, and it makes our egos feel better to think life is not fair. Our lives are not random events that occur for no reason. The realization that life is fair is realizing that life is a journey of experiences as a result of our karma and the lessons we came here to learn for the growth of our souls. Becoming conscious is to realize life is fair.

No one wants to hear 'life is fair,' there is a cause and effect, or action and reaction, for all our thoughts and deeds. Each of us is responsible for *all* that happens to us, both the good and the bad. The attitude 'life is not fair' is a fabulous excuse for us to not be responsible for our karma, our actions, or our lives. It is an excuse to justify our actions by blaming an outside source or others for our problems. Believing life is not fair is living in denial and playing the role of the victim. When you blame what happens in your life on others or outside sources, you become a victim of yourself, not others. Life only appears to be unfair when you are living unconsciously in the effects of your energy. When you live aware of your energy, you affect the outcome of your life. Your intentions and focus will produce the results you desire, whether you realize it or not.

Positive karma is *not* about being rewarded in life. Negative karma is *not* about punishment, debts to be paid, justice to be served, or a sentence that is issued. This is an illusion we have created. Good and bad things happen to all of us, and no one has a free ride. Everyone has trauma, turmoil, and pain in their lives at some point. It is how we handle the situations and what we learn that matters. We tend to learn our greatest lessons from our greatest hardships.

Karma is the energy of your being, and it creates the environment for you to learn life's lessons. You draw to you, due to your karma, the situations and opportunities necessary for you to learn. This includes both positive and negative experiences. Karma does not dictate your exact destiny, but it will affect how your life unfolds. The gift of free will gives you a say in your destiny due to the choices you make and the lessons you learn. You have the free will to choose how you deal with the karma you arrived with and the karma you create during this lifetime. As you learn, your karma will change, and if you choose not to learn, your karma will also change. It is up to you to choose the direction of your life, be it positive or negative.

As you become conscious, you will naturally be pulled in a positive direction as a result of striving to learn the lessons your experiences represent. You will begin to see random events, accidents, mistakes, errors, successes, and failures as opportunities to learn and grow. When you accept the outcome of any situation as positive, you affect the outcome, and the ability to learn.

The energy you are and the energy you create results in the causes and effects of your life. You have the ability to create positive and negative energy for yourself with the choices you make and the intentions of your thoughts and actions. You can accumulate negative energy and decrease the amount of positive energy, and you can likewise decrease negative energy by creating positive. This happens as you learn life's lessons and as you make conscious changes in your life.

Energy is like water, it seeks its own level. Energy draws to your life the situations necessary for you to learn life's lessons. This is why it is important to detach from a situation and realize you were drawn to a situation for a reason. As this happens, your life's experiences will become easier because you will be learning to deal with causes instead of focusing on and living in the effects. As you learn life's lessons, your energy will change and you will no longer be attracted to the same types of situations. This does not mean similar situations will not recur in your life. When a situation occurs that is reflective of a lesson you have learned, you have the free will to make the choice how you handle the situation, and in doing so learn even more.

How karma works exactly is beyond our comprehension. How God views our karma is something we have no concept of. We want to see a direct cause and effect, and place a value on the level of the action. We think stealing five cents is not as bad as stealing one million dollars. Are the two equal, or do they have two different values? Is the intention of stealing equal in all thefts?

Our ego sees the scenario as, you hit me, I hit you back, or I did this for you and now you owe me. This is not how karma works, and this is not how we learn. Karma is not about an eye for an eye or justice for any situation. As Gandhi said, "An eye for an eye would make us all blind." The ego seeks justice, and the soul seeks learning.

The karma you generate for yourself is based on not what you did or are doing, but on why. What were your intentions, motives, and reasons? Was it for personal gain, satisfaction of the ego, money, to cause harm, for revenge, out of disrespect, judgment, intolerance, control, and/or power, or was it out of love, integrity, respect, honesty, compassion, and/or forgiveness for the betterment of all concerned? Even while you are learning, you can still continue to create both positive and negative karma for yourself based on your thoughts, choices, and intentions.

Each of us has a moral sensibility or moral code within our souls. We know when we feel good about something, and when we do not. We also have a sense of when we are creating positive or negative results in a situation, and when it agrees with the inner moral code of our soul. The one thing we fail to realize is when we are causing problems for or harming any part of creation, we are harming ourselves as well. Ultimately what we do to someone or something, we do to ourselves because of the energy we create.

One of the obstacles creating an impact in the world today is people simply do not want to be responsible for their actions. No one wants to responsible for their fears, resentments, mistakes, or errors. We have become a society of victims living in denial and ignoring the causes. We want the bad and unpleasant things that happen in our lives to be the fault of or caused by someone else or an exterior source, and we usually want someone else to pay. It has to be someone else's fault. 'They' caused you to . . . , or whatever the excuse is.

It was the bartender who served you too many drinks that caused you to drive drunk and have an accident. It was the restaurant that served you the food, or the manufacturer of the food, that made you gain the weight. Not the fact that you chose to go to the resturant and chose what to eat, or that you went to the store, bought the junk food, and ate it. It was the cigarette manufacturer that caused you to smoke and get lung cancer, not that you were the one who smoked the cigarettes. It was your childhood. Maybe it was any number of things, but it is realizing no matter what happened, it was due to your karma or a choice you made, and is ultimately about a lesson you are here to learn.

The difficult part of learning the lessons is there is not a direct correlation between the event and the lesson to be learned. Until you detach, quiet your mind, go within, and ask what is really going on, you will not find the answers. The answers are there if you are willing to listen and go deep within your soul. You cannot deal with the cause of any situation by dealing with or reacting to its effects. When you deal with the effects of any situation, it is like closing the door to the barn after the horse is already loose. When you learn to deal with the cause, the effects will change. The soul has the answers and knows the causes, and the ego is only concerned with the effects. Once you know the cause, you can relate it to one or more of the values of the Truth and begin learning.

To realize the cause, you will need to take a step back by detaching, surrendering, and accepting what has happened so you can see the situation more clearly. This does not mean you will not experience the emotions of the situation. In fact, it is important that you do. The purpose of detaching is to become more objective by asking yourself why you feel the way you do, so you can reach the root of the cause. This is not easy to do. It may require time and distance from the situation and might even take years. It can be nearly impossible to realize the cause if you are stressed, overworked, too busy, too tired, frustrated, resentful, bitter, or angry. When you take the time to take stock of your life and put effort into being connected to your soul, it will be easier to be objective about your life, and the lessons will become easier to learn.

God does not punishment us. The Law of Karma is what we answer to. Through karma we serve ourselves our own justice and punishment in life. God does not lead us into temptation. We lead ourselves. Creating negative karma is actually us buying or creating our own trouble and problems. We are the ones who punish and test ourselves, not God. Of course, it is easier to play the victim and blame someone or something else for our problems, or feel we are being punished for being sinners, or we are not responsible for our lives.

You are responsible for your life, not just the good, but the unpleasant as well. Everything that occurs is due to the karma you came with or the karma you create. This may be a hard concept to understand and accept at first, but once you accept it and embrace it, you will discover a feeling of freedom and lightness to your life. You will release anger and frustration, become honest with yourself, and change your focus, your attitude, and your life. God and the Universe sees all and no acts go unnoticed, so you might as well be honest with God and yourself. You cannot escape your negative karma. The only escape is to realize it and change it to what you desire it to be.

The only way to repent, atone, or make amends for your mistakes and errors and change your karma is by learning life's lessons. Confessing and being sorry will only get you off the hook if you are truly affected and you strive to learn the lesson of the experience, and make the necessary changes in your thoughts and your behavior. Until you understand and learn the cause of your thoughts, emotions, feelings, intentions, and actions, you will not change your energy or its effects on your life. You need to deal with your feelings to understand why and what you are doing, before you will make changes in your thoughts and your life.

Life is not easy, and striving to live the values of the Truth can be challenging. We make it difficult by living the effects of our life's experiences, and not realizing the causes. Each of us has the free will to choose how we act, react, and feel, and each of us is responsible for the energy we create for ourselves. Becoming conscious and aware of the Truth, practicing the Golden Rule, and understanding the Law of Karma is realizing "life is fair." It is in striving to live the values of the Truth, that we heal our lives, and find the peace and love our souls seek. We already have God's unconditional love, compassion, and forgiveness. It is up to us to develop these qualities in ourselves by how we live our lives and how we interact with others.

The Energy of Our Being

We are energy beings. The energy of our being has more of an effect on our lives than most of us are aware of. What happens in our lives is about our energy and what our energy attracts to us, and not about luck, destiny, or fate. Our energy is very powerful, and the awareness and the focus of this power can change our lives. If only we were aware of the powerful energy each of us contains within our souls, the world and our lives would be much different.

The energy of your being is a balance, and it is not about being all positive or negative. Just like good and bad, each of us has both positive and negative energy as part of being human. The positive and negative aspects are necessary to learn life's lessons. Keep in mind that God and the Universe are absolute, constant, and consistent positive energy, and becoming one with this energy is the goal of your soul.

Becoming aware of your energy does not require you to be spiritual or conscious of your soul. You are free to use your energy in any way you choose. The illusion is, if your life looks good on the surface, your energy must be positive. An example of how this works is success in business. When someone's energy is intensely focused on success, they usually are successful. It does not mean they do or do not have negative energy, they are or are not spiritual, or they do or do not have integrity. Their focus is so strong on success that everything else is suppressed, and like energy attracts like energy. If someone's underlying energy is negative, their real qualities and intentions will surface at some point, but usually not the way we expect.

Energy is in a constant state of motion. We cannot see energy, but we know it is there. We easily understand this due to radio waves and wireless communication. We can feel when someone is happy, sad, or angry. Everything on this earth, from rocks to every cell of our bodies, is in a constant state of motion, and therefore, in a constant state of change. Our lives are in a constant state of change, and we must remain aware of our energy to stay in balance.

The energy of your being is like a magnet. You experience in your life what you attract to your life. When you are positive, you will naturally repel much of the negative. Creating positive energy in and around you is the key to having a fulfilling life. Creating negative energy in and around you will lead to a life of turmoil and dissatisfaction. This will occur even if you are not aware of what you are creating for yourself. What you draw to your life is due to your energy, and it is about learning life's lessons. You will continue to draw to you that which you need to learn, and learning is a continuous process that does not stop. When you do not learn from your life's experiences, you are actually struggling with yourself. Life is not about bad luck or punishment, it is about learning.

Becoming conscious and connected to your soul is to become aware of your energy. When you are aware of your energy, you will realize what kind of energy you are projecting. To do this you need to get in touch with your emotions and feelings and deal with why you feel the way you do. When you realize your energy is directing your life, you can know it, feel it, own it, embrace it, and change it. When you are aware of your energy and are true to yourself, you can create anything in your life you want.

Negative energy is like a ball and chain. You drag it everywhere you go, it affects everything you do, and it creates difficulty in every step. Negative energy closes the doors to your soul, creating darkness, and allows you to ignore the light of God. When you live in the darkness of your soul, you are not really living. This is why when you open a door to your soul, allowing light to shine, you feel born again; each time you open another door, it feels like new birth.

Changing your energy will affect everyone around you. The changes you make will affect how you interact in every aspect of your life. When you change your energy, you will attract to you that which you are becoming and repel that which you no longer are. Know you still have the ability to be attracted to your old energy, due to the comfort of its familiarity, and this can be confusing. When you realize this, you will see your old ways more clearly and this will enhance your ability to learn even more.

Once you become aware of your energy, you will not want to be around anyone or anything that robs or drains your energy. Be aware there will be people in your life who will drain your energy if you allow it. You must constantly be aware of the energy around you to avoid the negative. Think of it as if you live in an area where every morning, before you put your boots on, you need to shake them to remove any bugs that might have crawled in overnight. Keep in mind no matter how positive your energy is there will be times when the energy that comes toward you, or that you become involved in, is negative. Being aware allows you to choose to walk away, see it as a wake-up call, or use it as a reminder to get back on track. What you do not want to do is take on someone else's energy and relinquish your own. Anything that drains your energy will keep you from realizing your true self. This is why self-esteem is so important. Do not judge others who are not at, or are no longer at, your energy level. Those which you repel should not be seen as bad or negative, just not on your frequency.

As you become more aware of your energy, do not be naive enough to think you can ward off all obstacles in life and take unreasonable risks. When your energy is more positive than negative, you will still have things happen that are unpleasant. You will still make mistakes and errors, have successes and failures. You will still experience personal tragedies. Our life path is about learning and it can take many forms. Becoming aware of your energy is affected by your attitude. It is how you view life's experiences. It is realizing the negative energy of fears, stresses, and conflicts are like a poison if you allow them to become part of your life. To keep your energy positive and at as high a frequency as possible, you will need to be aware of the energy around you and your ego at all times. It is like staying in shape. When you stop exercising, your fitness level will decrease.

When you live in the present moment, know your energy will take you where you focus and the future will be as it should be, no matter what you are experiencing. When your focus is on the past or the future, your energy will be misdirected and you will remain stuck in life. Learning and growth occur when you live in the present moment and continue to move forward consciously in your life.

When you are conscious, you will give your energy genuinely and freely, and you will get back the energy you give and more, only you will not know how or when you will receive it. If you have the attitude you are owed for what you give, you will not actually be giving, but depleting your energy and creating negative energy. The positive energy of your soul gives, receives, inspires, radiates, and empowers without any loss to your being. Negative energy is needy, and it takes and drains your energy and the energy of others. As you advance consciously, not only will your positive energy increase, but you will also have more energy to give to others and create change in the world.

Our energy links us to each other like electricity. As you advance consciously, your positive energy will increase in amount and in frequency. The earth, environment, and the entire population is affected by the energy levels of those living on this planet at any given time. Our energy creates what happens in our lives. We are all one and our souls are all interconnected.

We are living in a time of great change. The turbulent world we live in today is a result of the energy of our greed, and lack of regard for others and the planet. It is up to us to balance our own energy and that of the world. All energy from God and the Universe is positive. The negative energies that exist are those which we create ourselves. We have the ability to change the world by changing our focus and our energy. The greatest energy we possess is love and its qualities of integrity, humility, peace, compassion, and forgiveness.

15

Life's Lessons

We are here to learn from our experiences. Life's experiences are for the purpose of learning life's lessons and the growth of our souls. The lessons each of us are here to learn for this lifetime were agreed upon before we were born. Life's lessons are about learning one or more of the values of the Truth. Human life and all that seems so important on the surface is just an illusion. The reality of life and what matters is love. We are here to learn love, and all of life's lessons lead to learning love, which is to learn the values of the Truth. Realizing this is to embrace life and strive to live authentically.

Life's experiences are the results of the karma we bring to this lifetime, the karma we create due to the choices we make, and the intentions of our thoughts and actions. Life's lessons are learned from the experiences of our mistakes, errors, successes, and failures. All of life's lessons lead to learning the values of the Truth, and the values of the Truth are the *cause* of our experiences.

Life's lessons are not about punishment, guilt, or shame. When your efforts are sincere, all choices are right. In some cases, when you make a choice you feel is right and it turns out to be not what you expected, know the outcome is part of the learning process. Life's lessons are learned from living life, and this includes the positive and negative experiences. The journey is about doing your best to learn and live the values of the Truth, and that you try. Know success is in the trying.

Life lessons are about experiences, not about winning or losing. Life is not a contest. The need to win is really about seeking approval and validation from others, and feeding the wants and needs of the ego. We know lessons are not about winning or losing, but about the experience. We realize this, so why don't we live it? The answer is simple, we get caught up in our ego-minds, performing like puppets dancing on society's strings.

Life's problems are created when you become involved in the effects of a situation and not in learning the cause. You create problems when you try to control or manipulate your life and the lives of others, when your life is about what you think you should be getting or what you think you are owed, and/or when your identity is based on the material world. Life's problems only exist in your ego-mind. When you create problems for yourself, you are simply contaminating your life by creating pain, stress, frustration, and negative energy. This is a result of living in the *effects* of your experiences, and not dealing with the *causes*.

It is by being connected to your soul that you relate the *causes* to the values of the Truth. Before the causes can be related to learning the values of the Truth, the cause must be related to the human side of your life. When you relate the cause to the human experience, you will need to deal with the emotions and feelings related to why you feel the way you do. Learning is seeing our experiences as they relate to our souls, not as they relate to our egos.

To understand how learning the values of the Truth is a result of what you feel, consider the following example. When you do not value or respect yourself as a person and you are treated this way by others, you will feel resentful, hurt, and devalued. When you deal with the feelings, you may blame how you feel on a past experience, such as someone telling you that you would never amount to anything. When you relate the cause to a life experience that is at the root of your feeling, you will be able to take responsibility for what you feel. Realizing the cause of your feeling as it relates to your human side is the first step to healing, and going within your soul is the next step. Going within is realizing you need to learn love or one of its qualities.

The journey of learning life's lessons is like climbing stairs. You have to climb each flight to reach the next level, and the journey of life is not always a continuous upward process. It is possible to advance as well as regress, depending on the choices you make. At any given time you can choose to climb the steps one by one, take several steps at a time, or make the choice to walk or run. As you climb, it is completely normal to trip, stumble, fall down a step or two, or more. When this happens, you need to pause, detach, and realize there is a lesson to be learned. Be patient, this usually takes time. It can take an instant, a day, a week, a month, many months, years, or even most of a lifetime. Realize you may need to repeat the same steps over and over again as you learn. If you become resentful, bitter, or unwilling to moving forward because of your fears, you will remain stuck in life, repeating the same mistakes and errors over and over again. As you climb the stairs on your life's journey, move at your own pace, with desire and determination. Travel your journey at your highest potential, and your life will be satisfying and whole, no matter what happens.

Once you learn a lesson, you will not repeat it unless you choose to. But, the values of the Truth are not something you learn once, and then you have no more to learn. As you advance in consciousness, you will uncover new lessons that will bring more meaning to the lessons you have already learned. This is the result of peeling away the layers of your emotions and feelings. You may think you have learned forgiveness, and then something will happen that will take you to a new level of understanding. The learning will continue to increase in depth and meaning throughout your life. The more you learn, the more you will realize there is much yet to learn, and this in itself is humbling.

The experiences of your life are telling you what you need to learn. It may be forgiveness or humility or compassion or peace or integrity, all of which lead to learning love. Which value or values you want to work on is up to you to decide. Keep in mind all the values are interconnected. God did not intend this to be complicated. So, in learning one, you are actually learning the others as well. When you focus on learning the values of the Truth, you will learn what you came here to learn. When you consciously take responsibility for your life and go within, you will realize the circumstances of your life are about learning, and this is when you will realize learning the values of the Truth is the cause of your life's experiences.

It usually takes a painful experience, or hitting bottom, to start the process of learning. We are so busy, that until we are forced to take stock of our lives, we do not realize what is important. Life's events are meant to transform our lives. Times of crisis and great emotional pain are when we go deep within our being to search for answers. It is not uncommon to hear people say that a severe illness or traumatic event was the best thing that ever happened to them. It is what it took to get their attention and to discover what really matters (the values of the Truth).

One way to take stock of your life is to consider if you were to face death today. Would you be at peace knowing you were leaving this earth? Would you be at peace knowing you had lived your best life? What would your response be? This is no time to say, I wish I had, or I was planning to . . . . The real question is *how* are you living your life? Are you living your life with love, integrity, humility, peace, compassion, and forgiveness? Are you honoring yourself and others? Are you living at your highest potential for the betterment of yourself and all mankind? Are you living with passion, fulfilling your dreams, or are you still waiting?

Death is part of life no one likes to think about, so we live in denial of its reality. Why are we so concerned about the longevity of life, and rarely concentrate on the quality of our lives? Why is our focus on the superficial, materialistic values of human life, rather than on what really matters? Why is it in death we *do not equate* money with the value of life, but in life we *equate* money with the value of our lives?

It is important to keep in mind we are human, and we need to allow ourselves to be human. We are going to make mistakes and errors, have successes and failures. In fact, we are supposed to, it is part of the learning process. Realize to err is human. We would not learn from our experiences if life was handed to us on a silver platter. If this were the case, we would not be here. Each of us learns in our own way and in our own time. Each of us has good sides, bad sides, and many sides in between that help us to learn.

Mistakes and errors are very humbling when you are honest with yourself. No one has an easy life, and all of us make mistakes. All of us live in glass houses with skeletons in our closets. Do not beat yourself up over the past or punish yourself for the mistakes and errors you have made. Learning is to know better. The more you learn and the deeper you dig, the more you receive. Learning life's lessons is a continuous, lifelong process. Have patience, be accepting, and embrace any and all progress that you make. Every little bit counts volumes and goes a long way toward opening the doors of your soul. When you realize life's experiences are about learning, you will no longer judge or criticize others for their mistakes and errors. You will realize everyone is here to learn just as you are, and you will allow yourself and others to change.

Life's lessons are not learned in theory or acquired through knowledge. Learning is accomplished by living and being, and applying the knowledge to your life as you live. You cannot learn love (or any value of the Truth) unless you live love. Living a conscious life from within your soul is challenging due to the distractions of the ego and dealing with material life. To cross the bridge from theory and knowledge to learning, requires desire, courage, and a continuous effort.

Life becomes easier when you learn to view all that happens with a positive attitude. Many times the success of learning is in the attitude. When you view your experiences with understanding, acceptance, love, integrity, humility, compassion, and forgiveness, you will learn. This will take the sting out of the painful experiences, and allow you to learn and move forward. The pain of any situation is only as devastating as you allow it or want it to be. Depending on your attitude, your life experiences can either make you rich in positive energy or poor in negative energy. When you see life as a journey of learning, life becomes freer and simpler.

As you learn, you will look back at your life and understand what you went through was for the purpose of learning. You will realize what you thought was an important event, as it related to your material life, was really about the lessons you are here to learn. You will realize suffering and unhappiness is a choice. You will look back at your life without bitterness or regret, and be thankful for the lessons you learned and how they have shaped your life.

No one but you can make your life work. It is your responsibility. Welcome all the successes and failures into your life, since both are very valuable. It is the cause of the situation from which you learn, not the situation itself. What you may have felt was a failure or bad experience is often one of life's best wake-up calls and an opportunity to learn some of life's greatest lessons. As you progress on your journey, you will come to realize it is in living life and dealing with life that you learn.

Thoughts, Emotions, and Feelings

You are your thoughts. Your thoughts affect your attitude and your energy. When the values of the Truth are at the base of your thoughts, the wants and neediness of your ego will be suppressed. Your approach to life will change and you will be more aligned with your soul. This will help you to follow the intuition of your soul, fulfill your life's purpose, and learn the lessons you came here to learn.

It is your thoughts that create your emotions and feelings, and being in touch with your emotions and feelings is to realize your true thoughts. Getting in touch with your emotions and feelings can be difficult unless you take responsibility for them. Being in denial or not being in touch with your emotions will keep you from seeing situations clearly, and will allow your ego to run your life. Anything that stirs your emotions is a message meant to get your attention. Your emotions and feeling are not about the specifics of a situation. They are about the lessons you need to learn from the situation.

When dealing with your feelings, keep in mind you are dealing with your karma and what you agreed to learn in this lifetime. Learning to feel is learning humility, compassion, and forgiveness. Give yourself permission to feel and express your emotions and feelings, so you can feel without barriers. This will happen if you quiet your mind and let go of your ego. Learning to really feel is difficult for many, since many do not realize it is necessary to focus inward. Relying on the knowledge within your soul is necessary to learn the meaning of your thoughts, emotions, and feelings, and to learn the meaning of your life. As you deal with your thoughts, emotions, and feelings, you will uncover their causes, and you will discover that all the causes are related to learning the values of the Truth.

The purpose of experiencing emotions and feelings is for learning and growth. This is why we experience such a wide range of emotions and feelings from absolute bliss to total despair. Dealing with your emotions and feelings is to realize all your positive and negative qualities. Give yourself permission to feel, and realize it is a necessary part of the learning process. When you learn to feel from within your soul, life will become easier and make more sense. You will be driving your emotions and feelings, instead of your emotions and feelings driving you.

Learning any task requires desire, time, dedication, and commitment. Dealing with your emotions and feelings will require taking time to focus on what you are feeling so you can realize the cause. When you focus on learning to deal with your emotions and feelings, you will need to trust what you feel. Be patient with yourself, and focus on being loving, compassionate, and forgiving. Do not just focus on your negative emotions, although these are the ones that usually surface most often and need the most work. The positive emotions are important as well, and lessons are learned from both.

Thoughts are at the root of all your emotions and feelings. The thoughts you have in your subconscious are reflected in how you live your life. Many go through life blindly, not realizing the impact their thoughts have on their lives. The purpose of our lives is for the growth of the soul, and growth occurs when you align your thoughts with the values of the Truth. When you are conscious and exercising your free will, you will be an active participant in the changes of your life. Changing your thoughts is a process that must begin with you. The most common way to avoid connecting with your emotions and feelings is by being caught up in the material life of overworking, overeating, overspending, overdoing, taking drugs, drinking, etc. When you bury your life in distractions, you merely cover up your emotions and feelings and do not cause them to disappear. Changing your thoughts requires taking time to get to know yourself so you can understand why you feel the way you do. When you know what you really feel and why, you will be able to deal with your thoughts and change them.

When changing your thoughts, you will need to feel,

believe, and live the emotions and feelings of the new thought. Changing your thoughts is like changing a habit. When deciding to change your eating habits to lose weight and keep it off, you will need to change your behavior. Changing old habits and patterns and reprogramming does not happen overnight and can be a struggle unless you are committed and focused. Changing your thoughts will require conscious deprogramming and reprogramming of the thoughts in your subconscious mind. Making changes in your life is not easy. The life you are currently living is familiar, whether it is positive or negative, and change is always unfamiliar.

Each of us is responsible for our thoughts. The ones we are born with, the ones we create, and the thoughts we are certain must have come from someone or somewhere else. Each of us is responsible for our internal dialogue, no matter what circumstances created it. You may have been called names, been a victim of a crime, felt unloved as a child, or are just unhappy with who you are, and as a result you feel emotionally wounded. Your wounds are about your karma and the lessons you are here to learn. You are the only one who can heal your wounds, no matter how they happen. When you realize you are responsible for all that happens in your life, your life will change.

No one changes until they are ready. The desire and intent to change must come from within or the change will be temporary. All of us want our lives to change for the better. Changing your life is changing your thoughts, and this must occur within your subconscious mind. When you find yourself thinking negative thoughts or being controlled by your ego, no matter what, never feel guilt, shame, or punish yourself. Have patience and try to stay focused on the values of the Truth. Every time you have a negative thought or feeling that does not align with the values of the Truth, realize it, feel it, and take the time to deal with it. Release a negative thought as soon as possible and replace it with a positive value as soon as you can.

Life is a series of events and situations, and changing your thoughts involves peeling away the layers of your emotions, and feelings. When you ask yourself why you feel a certain way, you will know why within your soul, but you may not be ready to acknowledge what you feel due to the fears of your ego. You will need to be honest with yourself before you will accept what you feel and change what you feel.

Love is life's greatest lesson. The inability to love others and yourself is blamed on many of the difficulties of life. A difficult and unloving childhood is often blamed for why someone's life is not working. Even if your childhood was difficult or even terrible, it is up to you to realize your childhood was about lessons you need to learn or you would not have had the experience. Once you reach this realization, your attitude and your way of viewing your life will change, and you will begin to heal, learn, and grow. Ultimately, it is up to you to deal with your life.

Learning to love all that you are will help you to change your thoughts. When you love yourself, you will no longer feel resentful about why you feel the way you do, and you will deal with your thoughts and feelings with compassion and forgiveness. You will embrace the parts of you that are hurting, and realize you can make any change you desire when you do the work.

When changing a thought, you will need to feel and live the new thought. You will need to live the new thought until it becomes part of your life. Repetition is the mother of learning. Changing a thought may require you to fake it until you make it, but do whatever it takes. Occasionally something will happen that will cause you to change instantly, but other changes will take time.

Think of changing your thoughts as planting seeds in the garden of your life. You get to choose the seeds you plant. Some seeds grow very quickly, some will take weeks before you see any growth, and others may lie dormant for many years. The thoughts (seeds) you plant will become who you are. Daisy seeds grow daisies. How you care for your garden will also affect its growth. The more care and positive energy you fertilize it with, the more positive your attitude will become. Keep in mind there will always be weeds from your ego and outside influences. It is up to you to deal with them and remove them.

Words are the seeds that create our thoughts. Words are energy and all energy is powerful. We do not grasp this concept because we do not realize the energy that is involved. Words become our thoughts when we feel them, believe them, and live them. The thoughts and beliefs we have about ourselves become who we are. Our thoughts dictate our life's experiences and how we handle them. If you truly believe and feel any realistic thought with desire and conviction, it will come to be. When you give a person a sugar pill (a placebo) and they believe it is going to help their symptoms, they get better. Your thoughts will attract to you that which you focus on.

Be careful of the words you use to express your thoughts. Negative words and thoughts will create a negative energy, just as positive words and thoughts will create a positive energy. Avoid thinking negative thoughts and using negative words in your conversations to describe yourself and others. When you think negative thoughts in your mind and use negative words to describe your thoughts and feelings, your energy will become negative. Not that you will be able to be positive all the time, but your internal dialogue is important. Change the energy of your thoughts and change your life.

Create balance and harmony in your life by meaning what you say and saying what you mean. Do not worry how others interpret what you say when you are being true and honest. Realize each of us sees and interprets things differently due to our different levels of consciousness and experiences. Each of us sees the world and ourselves with our thoughts. You are the only one who thinks your thoughts and interprets how you see things. You may think you know what someone else is thinking or feeling, but you never really do.

When your ego is running your life, it is possible to be consumed by your emotions and feelings and to live their effects. Becoming conscious is learning to deal with your emotions and feelings and striving to keep your thoughts in line with the values of the Truth. Changing your thoughts is not just about removing the negative and replacing it with positive. It is about changing your life to feed your soul and fulfilling your purpose in life.

Look to the values of the Truth for the answers and solutions to all your life's experiences. Accept you are human, and learning is a continuous process. Change will become easier when you focus on your life from within your soul. When you follow the intuition of your soul and divine guidance, you become the co-creator of your life. Embrace the Truth and you will embrace life, and all that happens, with positive energy and a positive attitude.

Fear

Fear is the opposite of love, not hate. Hate is one of fear's many qualities. Fear is negative energy that produces negative results. Love is positive energy that produces positive results. Fear keeps you repeating mistakes and errors in life, and love allows you to learn from your mistakes and errors. Fear is our greatest obstacle to learning love and life's lessons.

We are not born with fears. We are born with the will to survive, and the natural instincts that keep us safe. Fears are not about keeping us safe. Our natural instincts, intuition, and common sense are what keep us safe. Fear is created by our egos as a result of our insecurities, vulnerabilities, doubts, and lack of self-esteem. Fears are the anticipation of what might happen, which creates the conditions for what we expect to happen, and result in self-fulfilling prophecies. Fears keep us from living life. Fear, worry, and anticipation exist only when we are living in the past or the future, not the present moment. Living in the present moment is one way to deal with fear.

Fear reflects the qualities of hate, doubt, dishonesty, lying, greed, neediness, blame, violence, vengeance, hostility, abuse, resentment, bitterness, cruelty, ignorance, etc. The emotions and feelings associated with fear are anger, guilt, shame, anxiety, agitation, stress, worry, tension, depression, apprehension, rejection, pain, frustration, confusion, panic, dread, terror, sorrow, pity, etc. The results are judgment, intolerance, bigotry, jealousy, gossip, ridicule, unhappiness, lack of contentment, lack of self-esteem, and dissatisfaction with life. It is important to feel and understand these qualities, emotions, and results when they occur, so that you can deal with their causes and release them.

Fears are learned as a result of negative programming. When your fears become your emotions and feelings, you become a victim of yourself, which causes self-inflicted punishment. When you are a victim, you avoid dealing with the causes of your fears, and you live your life caught up in their effects. Living the effects of fear attracts drama, frustration, pain, and torment to your life, even though you may not realize it. Being a victim creates negative energy, no matter what the cause. The negative energy of your fears attracts more negative energy and perpetuates the cycle.

Fears are created in our minds by feeling fear of life, death, failure, success, change, etc. Some of our fears are the result of actual life experiences that we have been involved in or witnessed, and others are simply from the negative influences that have become part of our lives. Our lives are full of negative influences. Just watching the evening news can cause anyone to fear just about everything. Why does bad news sell better than good news? When we allow what is going on around us and in the world to affect us negatively, our lives become fear-based. Fears create problems, complications, and conflicts in our lives by creating negative energy and drawing negative energy toward us.

Fears drain your positive energy. Fears are what stand between you, your dreams, and the life you were meant to live. Fear keeps you from knowing love and creates a barrier to knowing God's love. Fears close the doors of your soul and are nothing more than darkness. To remove the darkness, you simply need to turn on the lights by opening the doors to your soul with positive energy. Releasing fears is the key to freedom in life and learning love. Fear has no real power and fear only has the power you give it. Love is the only real power that exists. Love creates positive energy and dissolves fears. Love knows no fear, and love is the courage to live your best life.

Many times our fears cause us to become someone we are not, in order to please others, or to be accepted in hope of being loved. When we act out of fear, we forget who we are and become caught up in life, ending up dissatisfied. Fears cause us to make decisions based on our egos, and not the intuition of our souls. We select careers to please others, we get married for the wrong reasons, and we attempt to overcome our fears with money, possessions, and achievements. We hide from our fears in the melodrama of the life we create for ourselves.

The ego is the obstacle to overcoming fears. The ego makes everything in the material world seem important, and the ego does not have the ability to face fears. Self-doubt is the most common fear of the ego, and it is the fear that causes the constant struggle between our unconscious and conscious lives. Fears keep us from being able to detach and think clearly. Fear prohibits our ability to believe in ourselves and be true and honest with ourselves.

The power to overcome your fears and silence the ego comes from within. The process is to become conscious, let go, and surrender. It is by being conscious that you are able to replace negative thoughts with positive thoughts, as a result of dealing with your emotions and feelings. The power to do this is found in love, faith, self-esteem, and the values of the Truth. As you learn to deal with your fears, keep in mind no matter how conscious you become, fears will still surface and consume your life from time to time. When this happens, know it is part of the learning process.

When you are conscious and connected to your soul, you will deal with your fears. It is in dealing with your fears that you learn. As you learn, you will create fewer problems for yourself and not become absorbed in the problems of others by taking on their energy. The only fears that will affect your life will be the fears you allow. "There is nothing to fear but fear itself." When you face your fears with love, you will cause them to dissolve. Be patient. Dealing with some fears will take more time than others. When you are conscious and committed to living the values of the Truth, you will release your fears as you learn.

Judgment and Intolerance

Judgments and intolerances are barriers to learning life's lessons. Judgments are the result of our views of someone or something based on the opinions of our egos. We are not here to question or judge the role of others. We are here to learn, and learning from our relationships is one of the ways we learn.

Judgment is the disrespect we have for ourselves and others that creates negative energy and harmful effects. Judgment and intolerance are the prejudice and hostility we have toward others due to our fears and insecurities, and due to not allowing others to be who they are. All judgments and intolerances are created by the ego-mind and are not of the soul. All judgments and intolerances create negative energy.

Judgments and intolerances are due to a lack of self-esteem, the fear of being judged, and the fears resulting from learned behavior. When you do not honor yourself, judging others is an attempt to make you feel better about your life. The judgments you make about others reflect back to you that which you are. Judging others is judgment of one's self and the result of being a victim of your thoughts. The judgments you cast upon others are a mask for the cause of your fears.

We tend not to judge others with whom we share a common experience, even when we would have otherwise. This is often the case when a common problem or pain is shared. This is evident in many twelve-step groups where, in most cases, there is not only support for the problem, but lessons in the values of the Truth as well. Being involved in a support group is the reality that cancer, alcoholism, etc., makes no judgments about whom it affects. It affects everyone, no matter what their role in life, how much money they have, the color of their skin, their culture, or their religious faith.

Why do we place labels on others based on their appearance, lifestyle, culture, and beliefs? Why do we not accept that which is not familiar to us? What are we really afraid of? Maybe we were meant to be different, based on our individuality, color, nationality, and faith. If we were not meant to be different, we would have not been created this way. Could it be we were created this way to make us realize we are not that different and that we are all one? Each of us is different and unique, yet we are all very similar.

Think for a minute. If each of us were to put on special glasses that made us all look the same, wearing the same clothes and speaking the same language, how would we judge each other then? I am sure we would find something, but it would be more difficult. What we fail to realize is that we are all just human beings, no one is any better than anyone else, our day-to-day lives are very similar, each of us is here for a purpose, and none of us have the ability or the authority to judge anyone.

Our judgments of others are based on the exterior, materialistic values that have nothing to do with who we really are or what really matters. We have no idea who the true person is on the inside, and yet we continually judge the book by its cover. When we judge others, we fail to realize each of us has the light of God within our souls. Judging others is acting like a child instead of being a responsible adult. Judgment is the ego's way of making itself feel better, while not realizing the negative energy being created.

Have you ever met someone for whom you formed an opinion because of the way they looked, then changed your opinion once you got to know them? When you got to know them, you no longer judged them for what you thought you saw on the surface. You realize you like them for who they are, how they affect your life, and how they make you feel.

We are more alike than different, yet we use labels to describe each other. Labels are false images and illusions created by our ego. Labels can be positive or negative, but it is the negative labels that result in humiliation, prejudice, and intolerance. Negative labels are words that cause harm. It is not the words that cause the harm, it is the meaning given to the words, and how they are used, that causes the harm. Sticks and stones may break your bones, but words of disrespect cause harm. Humiliation is one of the harshest forms of judgment. Humiliation strips a person of their dignity. Whether you realize it or not, when you humiliate someone, you are humiliating yourself.

Judgment of ourselves and others is one of the most difficult obstacles to overcome in our society. We are constantly surrounded in our daily lives with sensationalism in the media that distorts what is true, creates gossip, ridicule, drama, opinions, and intolerances. We tend to thrive on all of this, so much so, we do not even realize we are creating a vicious cycle of negativity.

Judgment is placing our opinions on others. We need to realize each of us is here for a purpose, and each of us is on a different path and at a different level of consciousness. What someone is here for is not up to us to decide, and it is not up to us to judge their lives. Part of becoming aware of the Truth is to realize we need to allow others to be who they are, allow them to make their own decisions and live their own lives. The individual who does not judge others is the greatest inspiration to all mankind. The best examples to follow are the ascending masters.

Learning nonjudgment and tolerance teaches us to become individuals and to accept others for who they are. This is to respect others with understanding and compassion. Nonjudgment does not mean everyone will get along, but rather it is the ability to accept others for who they are and treat them with respect.

Nonjudgment and tolerance occurs when our opinions are not projected onto others. As humans, we have opinions, but it is what we do with our opinions that matters. Opinions are our impression of how we see things, and should not be used to judge or affect someone else's life adversely. Nonjudgment and tolerance occur when we deal with facts that are true. Facts and truths do not create judgments, they just are. When you deal with facts, honesty, and truth, freedom is the result. Opinions are not facts, and need to be seen as learning tools. Realizing the *cause* of an opinion will lead to learning the values of the Truth.

Nonjudgment and tolerance is love, integrity, humility, compassion, and forgiveness, and realizing we are all one. Making a conscious effort to change judgments and intolerances, that are a part of our society, is a matter of realizing the amount of judgments we live with daily, and how it adversely affects us.

Judgments are learned, we are not born with them. One Thanksgiving Day, when I was a volunteering at a crisis nursery, I was in a play area with six, ten-to-fourteen-month olds. Just about every race was represented. There were black, white, Hispanic, Asian, Middle Eastern, and Native American babies. The babies had no problems interacting with one another, with no notice or regard for any of the external differences between them. They just wanted to be loved and entertained. Babies are easy to love, and I found it very easy to love each one of them without a care as to race, color, or nationality.

The reality that we are all one struck me as I interacted with the babies. I asked myself, what if this were a group of adults? I knew not only their behavior, but mine, would be very different. I knew within my soul we are all one and understood that prejudice is a result of learned behavior from the ego's point of view, and yet I realized I still had fears regarding race. I felt very ashamed realizing I still had feelings of prejudice, knowing there was no basis, and that I thought I had dealt with and released the feelings of past learned behavior. What I experienced that morning was very humbling, took me to a new level of understanding, and changed my life. It is an experience I would recommend to anyone.

As humans we do not have the capacity to judge one another externally or internally. To be able to judge someone's interior, we would have to know and understand the entire script of someone's life, and this is not possible for us as humans. We really never know another person, what they really think, what their experiences have been, how they have been affected, how they really feel, or what their purpose in life is. Judgment is actually comparing ourselves to others based on our own past experiences, beliefs, and emotions, and it really has nothing to do with the other person. Even what we think we are able to interpret from the Bible or other sacred texts is still not sufficient for us to judge someone else's life.

We are accountable only to God. God is the only one with the ability to judge us and we should leave it up to him, since what we decide really has no bearing on anyone's soul. The only effect judgment has is the negative energy it creates for ourselves and others. God sees each of us individually as we truly are, as our souls, and not as our earthly bodies.

Becoming conscious and connected to your soul will give

you the wisdom to no longer judge, since the soul knows it does not have the capacity to judge. Letting go of judgment is learning the values of the Truth, which opens the doors of your soul and creates light, dissolving the darkness of judgment.

Relationships

The relationships we have with each other are important not only for how we affect each other, but also for what they tell us about ourselves. The people we meet, have contact with, and build relationships with enter our lives for a reason. Our relationships are mirrors of who we are, and it is how we learn about ourselves. Even when partners appear to be opposite on the surface, they are more alike subconsciously then we realize. Our interaction with others exposes us to our thoughts, emotions, and feelings, and all relationships have value whether they are positive or negative. It is by our interactions with others that we learn many of life's lessons and the values of the Truth.

Relationships are often difficult because we live in a society where we want someone else to fix our lives. When you search for someone to fix your life, you are drawn to someone who also needs fixing. A relationship based on need is relying on someone else to meet your emotional needs. This is an unrealistic expectation. Relationships based on need do not last, since no one is getting what they want or need. You cannot give what you do not have.

The relationships we say we want are relationships with unconditional love, mutual respect, and trust. This is what we want, but this is not what many of us reflect. Realize this is searching for love outside ourselves, instead of focusing on learning, knowing, and feeling love from within. The ego needs love, seeks love for itself from others, and confuses romantic love with what love really is.

Becoming an individual and gaining self-esteem is learning love. When you focus on the values of the Truth from within your soul, you will have the desire to be who you are and not what someone else wants or needs you to be. This does not mean you do not want someone in your life. It is realizing that needing someone to make you feel complete is not how it works. What works is entering into a relationship focusing on being a whole person. Gaining self-esteem by becoming conscious and connected to your soul is learning to become whole. When you are whole within yourself, you will give and receive freely. When you are not whole, you will take from others and they will take from you, but, oh, the lessons you can learn. Relationships are always successful, no matter how they end up, when you are able to learn.

When you lack self-esteem and are not an individual, you will sacrifice yourself in your relationships, due to being selfless. An example is when a mother cares for her family at the exclusion of herself. One day she wakes up to find herself in an unhappy marriage and family life, and realizes she does not even know who she is. This is also true for fathers who one day realize that they were a good provider, but they did not take the time to really get to know their children or maintain the relationship with their wife. When a mother and/or father has self-esteem, everyone in the family benefits. When you have self-esteem, you have the ability to care for others without sacrificing any part of your own well-being, and you enrich the lives of others you come in contact with.

Relationships are about learning. The issue is not whether the relationship fails or succeeds. Relationships are a result of like attracting like, and herein lies the lesson. The world is your mirror. The relationships you have with others reflect how you feel about yourself. Detach from the situation to see your relationships more clearly, and you will start to see yourself in others. As you gain a sense of yourself from within, you will gain confidence. The relationships you have with others will teach you many of life's lessons.

Soul Mates

Many are looking for a soul mate to make their lives whole and complete, so they can live happily ever after. This is not how it works. Relationships are about learning. Feeling whole and complete comes from connecting to your soul and your oneness with God as a result of becoming conscious.

We think of a soul mate as someone who makes us feel comfortable, and comfort is often confused with feeling complete. Many times what we consider a soul mate is not someone who will make our lives complete. Due to our energy, we are drawn to that which we are. Being comfortable with someone may be the result of the comfort zone of our ego or karma. In this case, what feels like a soul mate is actually not. We are creatures of habit, and what feels familiar often feels comfortable, whether it is positive or negative. Abused children are often drawn to abusive relationships as adults, because we tend to live what we know. A soul mate takes nothing and gives positive energy.

A soul mate is someone we recognize from within our souls. This is anyone who is connected to us at the soul level. This is more than someone we are comfortable with or attracted to. This is when you feel an instant bond and connection deep within.

Soul mates feed each other's soul. Soul mates gives freely, receives freely, takes nothing, and both lives are enhanced because of the relationship. A soul mate can be anyone, a friend, relative, lover, coworker, someone you met once, or anyone that you connect with.

Relationships change over time as you learn and grow. No relationship provides everything you need other than the relationship you have with yourself and God.

The Learning Process

I came across this story on the Internet:

Life in Six Chapters

I walk down the street...there is a hole in the street. I fall into the hole...but I do not know I am in it. Finally I see the hole and try to get out. It takes a long time to get out of the hole.

I walk down the same street...the hole is still there... I see the hole. I fall into the hole again...but I recognize where I am and I want to be out of the hole. It still takes a long time to get out of the hole.

I walk down the same street... the hole is still there... I see the hole and still fall into the hole again...it has become familiar... But I have learned how to get out of the hole and...get out of the hole much quicker.

I walk down the same street again...the hole is always going to be there in this street. I see the hole...and recognize it...and think fondly of it... but I think I do not want to be in the hole again. But I walk directly toward the hole and fall in again. I get out immediately.

I walk down the same street... the hole hasn't moved... I like the look of the hole. Yet I remember I do not want to be in the hole... I remember the feeling in the hole... I veer away... I walk around the hole and continue on my way.

I go for a walk.... I walk down a different street.

--Unknown Author

If you think about it, this story sums up the *process* how we learn life's lessons and change our lives.

Part 5

16

Becoming Conscious, The Connection

Each of us is born with the natural hunger to connect with our souls. Becoming conscious is becoming one with your soul and one with God. It is realizing you are a soul in human form, and discovering the difference between the consciousness of the soul and the unconsciousness of the ego. Consciousness is the result of taking time to address your life. How this happens is up to you. Each of us has the free will to choose the path we take.

Becoming conscious is realizing that you and you alone are responsible for your life. You have the gift of free will to make choices and the free will to change your life. When you accept responsibility for your life, you will realize all of your experiences are of your own doing, whether they make sense to you or not. You will accept things happen for a reason, and the growth and development of your soul is the reason. When you do not take responsibility for your life, learning life's lessons is difficult if not impossible.

When you search within for the connection to your soul, you will also seek inspiration, enhancement, and validation from outside sources. Know that outside sources provide inspiration, support, and information, but they cannot create the connection for you. Becoming conscious is like developing a talent. If you are driven and have the desire to develop a talent, you will accomplish more than someone who is naturally talented but waits for the world to give them their due. All the knowing and knowledge in the world will not make you conscious, you must do the work. You have the credentials. You have been hired for the job, but you have to show up for work and do the job if you expect to get paid.

Becoming conscious and connecting with your soul is only as difficult to achieve as you want it to be. The doubts, roadblocks, barriers, and traditional fearful beliefs about God are due to the ego and from learned behavior. Becoming conscious is like discovering the keys to your life when they have been in your pocket all along. Consciousness will allow you to place your ego in the back seat and trust your soul to drive your life.

Conscious individuals are a minority in our society and the world. They are the few who take the time to open the doors of their souls and become conscious. The natural ability is there for each of us. Consciousness is not about being special or chosen, it is about being humble and striving to live the values of the Truth for the betterment of not only the self, but for all mankind and creation.

Becoming conscious and connected to your soul is a continuous process, and even the slightest connection is significant. All it takes is a crack in the door to let the light shine through to start you on your way. Once the light starts to shine, the darkness will begin to fade so that you can see to find your way. The light will expose the Truth, and you will know it when you feel it. You will not be able to deny the presence of the light, but your ego can chose to ignore it. Give yourself the permission to silence your ego and connect with your soul.

As you grow consciously, you will learn to recognize and deal with your ego. When you realize the experiences that are a result of your ego, you will be on your way to dealing with your life. The awareness of your ego is the result of humility. When you become humble, you will recognize the parts of your life that your ego is affecting. Keep in mind, even when you are conscious and connected to your soul, there will still be the tendency for you to doubt yourself due to the influences of the ego.

When you are connected even a little, you will begin to see the world and yourself honestly. While this is humbling, it can also be hard to deal with. You will realize the difficulty of incorporating the values of the Truth into your everyday life. You may also feel you are struggling to live the values of the Truth, since you will still be making mistakes and errors. When this happens, remind yourself that you are here to learn and mistakes and errors are part of the process. Once you are aware of your soul and the part your ego plays, you will be humbled, realizing how easy it is to slip back into your old unconscious ways.

Becoming conscious takes practice and patience, and more practice and patience. Part of being patient is quieting your mind. When you are patient and your mind is quiet, the messages from within your soul will come through. You have to want this more than anything else in your life, and you have to be dedicated to doing the work. You will need to create a lifestyle to fit your conscious life, and allow your life to change as you grow.

Going Within

Going within is what is necessary to connect with your soul, become aware of the Truth, and discover who you are and what your purpose in life is. Going within is connecting with your feelings and realizing your karma and your ego play a major role in your life. When you are able to connect with what you feel, you will have the ability to change the thoughts in your subconscious mind. You will become empowered, knowing you have the free will to change your energy and change your life. You will begin to view situations consciously with love instead of fear. This will change your focus, attitude, and energy.

Going within is quieting your mind so you can hear the messages from within your soul. This is not something you can force, you have to relax and let it happen. If you try to force it, your ego will get involved and your mind will influence your thoughts. Going within cannot be rationalized or understood by the mind. Relax, be patient with yourself, and handle yourself with the care and love you would give to a toddler learning to walk. Be thrilled and embrace yourself lovingly with each step you take. Allow yourself to feel the knowing so you can become aware.

Connecting with your soul will require desire, commitment, determination, discipline, and focus, because you are living a human life. You will need to develop a positive attitude, be true to yourself, get in touch with your thoughts, emotions, and feelings, and remove any obstacles that stand in your way by simplifying your life. Going within and connecting with your soul will empower you, and enhance your life and your relationships in more ways than you can imagine. All solutions, healing, and joy in life occur from within as a result of connecting with the light, love, and positive energy of God.

Developing a positive attitude is realizing the power of your thoughts. This does not mean you will be positive all the time, but your underlying view of life will be. Having a positive attitude is not hiding from your emotions or feelings. It is how you deal with your experiences and the events of the world. A positive attitude is viewing life and your experiences from the values of the Truth, knowing all things happen for a reason and learning life's lessons is the reason. When you accept what happens in your life with a positive attitude, the outcome and the effects change. This will go a long way toward affecting your energy and the energy of the world.

Going within is difficult when you are caught up in the superficial, materialistic world, or when you are busy chasing your life. Simplifying your life will help you to become centered and focused. It is much easier to stay focused on what matters when you reduce the distractions, become an individual, and gain self-esteem. When your life is simple, detaching and dealing with your thoughts, emotions, and feelings will become easier. Simplifying your life will help you to realize many of life's problems and distractions are due to a complicated lifestyle and the involvement of the ego.

When you are connected with your soul, you will navigate through your life with the intuition of your soul and divine guidance. You will recognize messages from your soul and suppress the messages from your ego. Remember, the messages from the soul are definite, and the messages of the ego create doubt and confusion.

Going within and making the connection requires true desire. You must have the desire to access the awareness of the Truth and the light of God from within your soul. Once you access it, you will be able to acknowledge it and realize it. Once you have accomplished this, you will hunger for more as your life begins to change. You will search for more understanding and enhancement for what you are feeling.

Quieting Your Mind

Quieting your mind is necessary to connect with your soul and to surrender, let go, and live the Truth. When you are struggling and trying to manipulate your life, doubts and fears will keep you from quieting your mind. Going within and connecting with your soul is getting out of your head and into your heart-soul-spirit. Along with the desire, you will need to give yourself permission to let it happen. If you sincerely desire to become conscious and connected with your soul, it will happen.

The ability to quiet your mind is often referred to as meditation. Culturally we are not encouraged to connect with our feelings or our souls, and as a result we have become handicapped, living shutdown lives. Meditation is not about becoming a guru, monk, or saint. Meditation is focusing on your energy, communicating with your soul, and developing a peace and calmness that is the result of the love from within your soul. The purpose and objective is to become centered so can you silence your ego-mind and create a barrier to outside influences. Meditation is becoming focused from within your soul, silencing your ego and the human side of your being so you can listen to your soul and to God and the Universe.

Meditation is spending quality time with your soul and God. When your mind is quiet, the doors to your soul will open, creating more light and positive energy. Meditation can be accomplished in many ways, and there is no right or wrong way. The way that works for you is the way to proceed. You may even meditate in different ways at different times. Traditionally meditating is sitting quietly, but you can also meditate while being active. The goal is to quiet your mind at any time, no matter what is going on around you, or what you are doing.

It is helpful to understand what a quiet mind feels like so you can let it happen. The most common comparison is that of a long-distance runner. It is the feeling achieved beyond the threshold of pain when the running becomes effortless. You feel a sense of being out-of-body. This feeling can be achieved in other ways, such as any time you become absorbed in a task that allows you to step out of your physical mind and function effortlessly. This can occur when you are listening to music, gardening, cleaning, exercising, any activity that allows you to escape, feel calm, and not dwell on your physical being.

The traditional way to meditate is to focus on your breath by breathing slowly and deeply to achieve a calmness and detachment from the physical life. This is when you breathe in through your nose and your stomach rises as you inhale. Your chest needs to remain still. Breathing from your chest and/or with your mouth open will not have the same calming effect. To achieve the feeling, it is helpful to count as you breathe in and out for the first several breaths, or more if necessary. Breathe in calmly, slowly, and deeply through your nose while counting slowly to four, hold the breath for four counts, then breathe out slowly though your nose for four counts. This will help to slow your breathing and establish a rhythm. You will begin to notice a difference in how you feel as your breathing slows and becomes light and effortless. The calmness will be the quieting of your mind. Develop this technique as part of your life, so you can pause and focus on your soul effortlessly at any time. It is also a useful technique for calming and focusing when you are upset, frustrated, or anxious.

When you focus on quieting your mind, it is best to spend time alone with no distractions in a peaceful environment. One of the best places to spend time alone is in nature, even if it is just your backyard or the local park. If this is not possible, find a place in your home where you can be peaceful and comfortable with no distractions. For some, listening to gentle, soothing music or sounds, like the ocean, a waterfall, rain, etc., are helpful. Another way is chanting. Some find exercise helpful as they become lost in the rhythm of the movement. Something like walking, running, biking, or swimming, where the motion is constant, works best.

Quieting your mind is connecting with your higher conscious self so you can hear your soul, receive guidance, and become an observer of your life. When your mind is quiet, you will become an observer of not only your life, but the lives of others, and you will learn so much more.

Quieting your mind will become second nature once it becomes part of your life. Give yourself the permission to quiet your mind, make it part of your being, and the changes in your life will be amazing.

Letting Go and Surrender

Letting go and surrendering is realizing you are not in control, and you cannot do it alone. As humans we do not have the ability to complete the task by ourselves. To let go and surrender requires God's help. Realizing your oneness with God will lead you to letting go and surrendering.

Letting go and surrendering is allowing the human part of you to become vulnerable to your soul. It is the ability to silence your ego and release the attachments to your ego-based emotions and the unnecessary attachments to the physical world, so you can embrace life and learn the lessons you came here to learn. This is to release your fears, realizing they have no real foundation other than that which you give them. This allows you to identify with your soul, and lets your life unfold, as you learn each step of the way, living in the present moment. Letting go and surrendering removes expectations and allows you to focus on the values of the Truth.

Letting go is silencing your ego. This is releasing your fears and the guilt associated with negative self-images so you can gain self-esteem. Letting go allows you to get in touch with the thoughts, emotions, and feelings that are not only in your subconscious, but also within your soul. The act of letting go allows you to surrender, detach, and become responsible for your life.

Learning to let go is difficult because we place so much emphasis on who we are physically and little emphasis is placed on our souls. The image we have of ourselves revolves around our physical being, and this is not who we really are. To live from within our souls, it is necessary to let go and surrender.

Surrendering is inviting divine guidance into your life and living devoted to the Truth. This is giving up any part of your being that does not align with living the Truth. Giving up does not mean you are going to get rid of everything in your life or become weak and dependent. Giving up is releasing the will of your ego so you can align your thoughts with the values of the Truth and release the attachments to the material world that keep you from becoming aligned with your soul. This is getting your priorities in order and realizing the human experience is important for the lessons you are here to learn. When your identity is based on the physical world, it is difficult to live your life authentically from within your soul. Surrendering is living what matters by living your life from within your soul.

When learning to let go and surrender, think of it as being an actor. Letting go is what actors do to become a character, and in this case you want to become the character of your soul. Realize the human qualities of your personality will still come through, just as some of an actor's personal qualities come through in any part. When an actor is successful at playing a part, the part becomes more about the character (the soul) than about the person the actor is (the ego). They let go of their ego and surrender to become the character. Strive to become the character of your soul until it becomes who you are. Relax and allow the realization to occur.

If you do not understand the concept of letting go and surrendering, realize it is your ego that does not understand, not your soul. Take time to reflect on your life and realize how insignificant many things become with the passing of time. Look at the big picture of your life instead of just the snapshots, and this will help you to let go and surrender. This is one of the benefits of aging, the reality that our lives here on earth are really just a moment in the span of eternal life. Letting go and surrendering is to seize the moment of this lifetime.

As you let go and silence your ego, your soul will become the navigator of your life. You will rely on the intuition of your soul and divine guidance to inspire and influence your every thought and action. Be aware you will still regress back to the familiar ways of your ego from time to time. Understand this is because your ego has been in control for a long time, the ego is part of being human, and there will always be lessons to learn.

Learning to let go and surrender will not happen overnight. Letting go and surrendering is like changing a habit, and changing any habit takes time, discipline, and determination.

Letting go and surrendering is living in the present moment, leaving the past behind, and allowing the future to unfold. Do not become attached to a certain outcome in any situation or you will be controlling the process. Relax and let it happen; trust the outcome will be as it should be. Ask for guidance and be firm in your intentions and convictions. If you have doubts, you will affect the outcome. You might as well be honest with yourself. Remember, you can hide nothing from God and the Universe.

Many times, letting go and surrendering occurs as a result of hitting bottom. When life is difficult, we naturally turn inward. This is when we search for the meaning of our lives and ask for help. Support and divine guidance is always available to each of us, not only in times of need.

Letting go and surrendering is not sacrificing who you are, but becoming who you were meant to be. This is discovering your joy, passion, inner peace, contentment, satisfaction, and purpose in life. Letting go and surrendering is empowering, and removes the fears and uncertainties of life. When you are empowered, you will focus on the energy of your spiritual being, and your life will flow and change in many ways you never thought possible. The abundance of living a rich life will be yours.

Letting go and surrendering is realizing God is not only part of your life, but part of your being. This reality is not easy to understand, and living a life devoted to God is not easy in today's world. We want what happens in our physical lives to give us everything we need, but we are souls first and living from within our souls is the answer to a successful human life.

Living It

The turning point in consciousness occurs when your life is about living the Truth, and this is life's challenge. Living it requires you to apply the values of the Truth to your daily life. Many reach the point of knowing and realizing the Truth, but do not implement living it as part of their daily lives. This is living consciously on the inside while living unconsciously on the outside, and this can lead to feelings of being discontented and unfulfilled.

Living the values of the Truth is what feeds your soul. Nourishment for the soul is love. Love is realizing the light of God within, and this leads to honoring yourself and others. Honoring yourself leads to self-esteem and becoming an individual. Living to feed your soul is a matter of what you focus on. Your life is what you focus on, or it becomes what you focus on. Focusing is a matter of quality and not quantity. The soul knows it is the quality of how you live your life that leads to the quantity of your life. Focusing on living the values of the Truth is what gives quality and meaning to life and feeds your soul.

What you focus on is reflected in how you live your life. Stop and take a long look at your life and rank your priorities. Ask yourself some of these questions. What value do you place on your relationship with God? What value do you place on your health, sense of well-being, inner peace, satisfaction, and contentment? What value do you place on your family, job, material possessions, etc? Most of us, when we are honest, will realize what we say we value and how we live our lives are miles apart. Is the focus of your life what you value in life? Is what you value reflected in *how* you live your life? Are you living what matters? Is what you value feeding your soul, or feeding your ego? Anything can be justified by the ego, but the real question is can you justify it from within your soul?

Living it is realizing the gift of life, the gift of free will, and the knowledge of the Truth within your soul. It is living your life with the underlying positive attitude of living love as the basis for your thoughts, choices, and intentions. The easiest way to live the values of the Truth is to live with integrity and compassion as the focus of your life. When you live your life with integrity and compassion, then humility, forgiveness, peace, and love follow. Living it is not about being perfect. It is about striving to do your best. Success is in the trying. If your efforts are sincere, and you have the desire, you will accomplish more than you can imagine.

To live the Truth, it is necessary to remove the stigmas that you are not worthy and that the message is complicated. The message is simple and you need to allow yourself to see it that way. It is up to you to accept responsibility for your life, realize life is fair, and realize you are here to learn for the growth and development of your soul. Believe in yourself by living with passion and no regrets.

Becoming conscious, living the Truth, and living what matters requires you to apply yourself. You cannot just think about it or wish it to happen. You have to desire it, and *will* yourself to have the commitment and determination to take the challenge. If you want the results, you must do the work. The obstacles to becoming conscious are the doubts and fears of the ego and learned behaviors. To release your doubts and fears, you must quiet your mind, let go and surrender to God, and become committed to the Truth above all else.

Living it is realizing mistakes and errors are part of the process, and the success is in the learning. Life is not easy, but it will be if you choose to live it with an underlying positive attitude. This will allow you to embrace life and get you through the rough times. Go within and live what you feel from within your soul, without question. Allow yourself to change the course of your path at any time, and allow others to do the same. Live with integrity each moment of the day, and see yourself and others with compassion.

It is up to each of us to connect with our souls and become

one with God. Know you are loved, and know you always have the support of God and the Universe. Focus on yourself as a soul being, and live your life from within.

Relationship With God

Becoming conscious is not only inviting God into your life, but it is becoming aware that God is already part of your life and is within your soul. It is our relationship with God that gets us through life with feelings of inner peace, contentment, and satisfaction. A relationship with God is based on faith.

Developing a relationship with God has been made complicated by man's ego. The early rulers and religious leaders decided they were the only ones who could communicate with God, or Gods in some cases, and they were the link for the people who, of course, were unworthy. The tradition of feeling unworthy has carried through in our subconscious minds today. A relationship with God, the ascending masters, angels, or spirit guides needs to be from within your being, at a personal level, and this needs to be a comfortable relationship. You cannot develop a relationship with God unless you feel the comfort of his love from within.

Connecting with your soul is connecting to your oneness with God. Many of the religious faiths still teach that God is an outside source, and this has kept many from knowing his love. As humans we get hung up on titles. We feel because of a title, one person is more important than another. We think priest, reverend, rabbi, etc., are closer or more connected to God because of their title and role in life. A title and knowledge does not create the connection, or make anyone more special or more important than anyone else. This is not to diminish someone's role or title, but it is to realize each of us has the ability to connect and all of us are worthy of the connection. Are some more spiritually advanced than others? Yes. Does it mean that God loves them more? No. Each of us is simply at a different level of consciousness and not at a different level of importance. Someone who is spiritually advanced will be the last to say they are special. Spiritually advanced individuals are humbled by the experience, and usually feel a responsibility to inspire others. They want to give to others what they are experiencing.

When God is seen as an outside source, it is like having a crush on someone. The crush is meaningless, since no relationship exists. You cannot be in a personal relationship with someone you are not involved with. Love is a connection and a state of being from within, not something that exists outside of your being. To feel God's love is to know it, embrace it, and become familiar and comfortable with it, just as you would with any personal relationship.

Think of a relationship with God, for example, as an ideal relationship between a small child and a parent. In the ideal setting, the child adores the parent and sees them as larger than life. The child feels complete love and comfort, contentment, and security. The ideal parent provides the child everything they need to become the best they can be, and then they set them free to do so with love and support. Conversely, a small child does not want a parent they feel distant from, or only see occasionally. A child does not feel connected to a parent they are not sure of.

Feeling the connection with God's love is beyond what can be realized in words. God loves you more than you can imagine. A comfortable, close, personal relationship with God does not mean you lack reverence, honor, and respect. Will you be in awe of God's love when you feel it and know it? Absolutely. However, this will not be at the expense of becoming one with him or having a comfortable relationship. When you feel the wholeness of God's love from within your being, your life will change.

A comfortable relationship with God and the attraction to the knowledge of the Truth is natural for the soul. God does not want you to fear him, feel distant from him, or consider him out of your reach. If you feel unworthy or fear God, you will not be able to know his love. As you become connected to your soul, allow yourself to become connected with God in a comfortable way, so you can develop a sense of oneness. When you feel the inner beauty and energy of that which is love, you will know God's love.

Personal relationships are not only based on feelings, but on communication as well. Communicating with God is key to developing a close relationship with him.

Communicating With God

Communicating with God opens the doors to your soul and your life. When you communicate with God, he will communicate with you. When you communicate with the angels, spirit guides, or any of the ascending masters, you will be communicating with God, and when they communicate with you, God is communicating with you. Communicating with God can be in many forms, and you are free to choose the way. The two most common ways are prayer and meditation, but there should also be a third common way, a simple informal conversation where you simply tell God what is on your mind. How you communicate is up to you, what is important is that you do communicate.

Communication is not just what you verbalize, it is also what is within your thoughts. Your true thoughts are found in your subconscious mind, and these thoughts are more powerful than you think. They convey what you really think and feel. You may think you are asking for one thing, when your thoughts are saying something else. When you are in touch with your thoughts, emotions, and feelings, you will be sincere and honest in your communications.

A relationship is developed with God by communicating with him simply, honestly, and sincerely. Make this easy for yourself, since he already knows everything about you, why you are here, what your purpose is, and what your thoughts are. Do not be afraid to express how you really feel, no matter how happy or angry you are. To do anything else would not be true or honest. Being honest with God is being honest with yourself, and this will put you in touch with your true feelings and silence your ego. When you are not honest, it is you who are lying to yourself.

Many only communicate with God when they find themselves in a difficult situation, when they want something, are grateful for a miraculous event, or when in a formal religious setting. Communication is not about bargaining or formality, it is about seeking divine guidance in all you do. It is asking what it is you need to do, not what can be done for you. It is not about the answers you want, but listening for, and allowing yourself to hear, the answers you receive. This is the hard part. Many times we hear what we want to hear, and do not listen to what we are receiving. Realize this occurs when you are listening with your ego-mind.

The communication you receive from God may come to you in many different forms. It will come to you much the same way as intuition comes from within your soul. You may experience divine guidance through dreams, visions, spiritual experiences, etc. It can be conveyed through songs, conversations, by reading, etc., or it may be that little voice inside of you. Divine guidance is often received as a feeling you can explain no other way, but you will know it is true from within your being.

It is easy to misunderstand or misinterpret the divine guidance you receive. Many times it is because you are not patient and want the answers immediately, or you have not asked honestly or realistically. You may have influenced the message with the answers you wanted and actually ignored the answers you received. When you ask for guidance, your mind needs to be quiet so you can listen.

In developing a personal, comfortable relationship with God, become used to communicating with him as freely as if you were talking to your best friend. All you have to do is give yourself permission to do so. When you have a relationship with God, and/or the angels, spirit guides, and ascending masters, you will see your life more clearly. They are your best teachers. They will be there for you any time you want to talk to them, and they will never turn their backs on you, no matter what. It is you who will turn your back on them.

Your relationship with God is an open book, whether you realize it or not. If you had to live your life as an open book, what thoughts would you have and what choices would you make? The unknowns and stereotypes about God have been created by man's ego. God is love, and the relationship he has with us is one of pure, unconditional love. There is nothing to fear from God. Go within and know you are loved, beyond your wildest imagination, and you will have all the support you could ever want or need. God knows everything about you and is available to listen and support you at all times.

Communication is key to your relationship with God, but just like in life, it is also important to become a good listener so you become aware of his guidance.

Part 6

17

It Is Up to Us

None of what has been stated is anything that each of us does not already know. Why we are here is evident in our creation and in our will to live. When we are faced with our own mortality or the loss of a loved one, we quickly realize what matters. All of us know that love is what matters, but we do not live what matters. We only live what matters in those moments when there has been a wake-up call that gets our attention; then we return to our everyday lives and wonder why things are not working.

We are living in a great time of change. We are living lives of conflict, stress, and frustration in a complicated world of fear and anger. This has become the norm, but none of us really like it, and we wish it would change. The turbulence, stress, and unrest are all part of the changing times we are experiencing. Wake-up calls are occurring constantly for us individually, as well as the entire population. The Truth has started to surface and is being realized more and more. The Truth has always been there, but it has just been covered up by distortions, contradictions, and misunderstandings. The Truth is, and it cannot be altered. It is up to us to become aware of the wake-up calls and begin to live the Truth

The Truth is what will change our lives. The Truth

removes complication, confusion, and nonsense from our lives. We keep trying to solve the mysteries of life, and in the meantime our lives have become exhausting. Why do we continue to try to figure things out as if we have the ability to control life? Why do we make life so complicated? Why are we our own worst enemy? Why do we find it so hard to embrace what is within our souls? Why is the reality of the Truth and the concept of consciousness so hard to grasp?

When asked, most people would acknowledge things happen for a reason, and most acknowledge a higher power that is greater than all of us and is the reason for our existence. Life could be made simple by embracing and living the basics of the Truth. The simple laws of nature (cause and effect, and like attracts like) apply to our lives so clearly, yet we do not live as if they do.

Many think God is controlling what is going on in the world, and some even think we are being punished. Mankind has created the imbalance of energy that is causing the turbulence in the world today, not only in our lives, but in the environment. We are the ones who have created the imbalances and it is up to us to correct them. We have done more in the last two hundred years to destroy this planet than all the years before. We have come so far, but at what price? Not that advancements have not been helpful, but many have been without reverence. The world has become a neighborhood that needs to be cleaned up, renovated, and remodeled. Change is beginning to occur, and to know this is to understand there is a good reason for all the turbulence and unrest that is currently taking place.

The spiritual consciousness of the Truth is starting to surface and we will begin to see more loving and compassionate times come into being. We are already seeing the combining of eastern and western philosophies. The changing levels of compassion were demonstrated after 9/11. Races are combining and being accepted, due to marriages and births. We are realizing stress is causing many of our illnesses. Many are beginning to seek awareness of the Truth to make sense of their lives. Information is surfacing, and a large number of spiritually advanced individuals are here at this time, offering guidance and inspiration. None of this is occurring by coincidence; however, the changes are not going to occur overnight. In fact, it will probably take several generations depending on the collective energy of the world, but know that positive change will occur as the Truth becomes the focus and the energy of our lives.

Living the Truth is difficult when the focus of our lives is on the superficial, material world. The ego is one excuse, but it is more than that. It is our misguided focus and priorities. We have come so far, yet we do not focus on why we are here. We have received the message of the Truth from the ascending masters and we hold the message in high regard, but we fail to teach it and live it. We do not teach or live love, kindness, integrity, humility, compassion, or forgiveness as a society or population. We do not teach self-esteem or how to deal with our emotions and feelings. Women are allowed to have emotions and feelings, but we actually teach men to suppress their emotions and feelings. We are surprised when we are around a child with manners, and this has become the exception rather than the norm. We do not teach fitness and nutrition, and the result is many of our current health issues. We have neglected the health of our bodies and the health of our souls. We talk about all these issues and we know they are important, but until recently they have been ignored. We are starting to see awareness of these issues surface.

Living the Truth is a challenge because we have created an environment where spirituality, consciousness, and the Truth are not an obvious part of our lives. We have made the Truth complicated by analyzing and interpreting what we think is the Truth or what we want it to be. We search for answers when the answers are right in front of us. Simplifying our lives and living what matters, to open the doors of our souls is the answer.

We have been given this beautiful planet as a place for our souls to learn, grow, and develop. Many are waiting for God to come, to stand in judgment and change the world. God is already here. He is in the soul of each and every one of us. It is we who fail to realize his presence. The story of Adam and Eve describes human life. We have been given paradise in the form of this earth in all its beauty and wonder, and the gifts of life and free will. It is up to us to realize what we have been given and to choose to live the values of the Truth, or allow ourselves to be controlled by our egos and live our lives unconsciously. We are responsible for this planet and our lives. We can continue to destroy the earth and live lives in turmoil, or we can choose to live consciously. We have the ability to make this earth and our lives the paradise they can be. This is the ultimate challenge of mankind. Know that all things are possible in the presence of love.

We have been given everything we need within our souls. The ascending masters delivered the message of the Truth to us. The message taught by Jesus Christ and the others was clear and simple, and it is up to us to realize it. We only need to discover the knowledge within, begin to live the Truth, and change our lives and the world. It is never too late to become aware and change life completely, for the world and for ourselves. If we want the world and our lives to change, we have to change the effects by realizing and dealing with the causes.

Our souls have become hungry due to our complicated lives, and many are beginning to search for guidance and a meaning to life. Creating an environment to support a conscious lifestyle is what is needed. Becoming conscious happens individually, but we are, collectively, the human race. We are all one. We need the support of interacting with each other to create a conscious environment. Religions have had a great effect on mankind over the centuries, and they still can. The religious faiths of the world are in a position to affect the energy level of the world and our lives, and provide the environment for consciousness to thrive.

If the religious faiths of the world would focus on the Truth, which is at their foundation, and realize how similar all of us are, things could change. Religious faiths have become so caught up in themselves that they have forgotten their roots. If religious faiths would become about the Truth, and not about being a business or an institution that performs as if it is the Truth, great change would occur. Relinquishing the ego-based rules and doctrines that have distorted the Truth would benefit mankind greatly. Relevant rituals based in the values of the Truth would give religious practices new meaning. The importance and emphasis of all religious practices needs to be based on the soul, not on the rules and differences created by the ego. We need to respect all cultures and faiths, realizing our similarities, yet respecting the differences. We cannot expect everyone to be the same, but we can live together realizing the Truth, and what matters, is the same for all of us.

We need to put aside our differences and realize we are all souls here for the purpose of growth and development. I know this may sound unrealistic, but it is not. The Truth is what the ascending masters lived and taught. It is up to us to realize it. It has been said the meek shall inherit the earth. The ego-based individuals see the conscious individual as meek. Living the Truth has the appearance of being meek. It is up to us to realize the power in the Truth and change the world.

The message of the Truth is completely positive. It is up to us to remove the negativity of the nontruths created by man's ego. This will require changing thousands of years of tradition, but it is a change that needs to occur. A very effective way to create change and teach the Truth is through religion. I would encourage all leaders and followers of the many faiths to make the changes and get back to the basics of teaching and practicing the positive values of the Truth, and inspire all to become conscious. This would change the lives of many and change the world we live in. Change is going to occur whether we want it to or not. We can choose to be a part of the change and create a positive conscious environment, or we can choose to let the current effects create an environment none of us want.

Education is the key to changing the world. We need to develop programs that inspire self-esteem and creativity. Our focus needs to be on living what matters and becoming passionate about life. The values of love, integrity, humility, peace, compassion, and forgiveness need to be taught as the focus of our religious faiths, in our homes and schools, through the media, and as part of our everyday lives. It is up to us to make the values of the Truth a priority in how we live our lives.

During my adult life, I have attended mass very infrequently. Some years ago, I attended mass with my family. I was surprised that the words and the routine had not changed. The one thing that affected me was at the end of the mass. The final words that I had heard so many times, "Go in peace to love and serve the Lord," caused me to pause. I stopped and looked around, and saw on the faces the expression, "Well, that's over with, I'm good for another week," that I'd seen so many times before. Just imagine how different the world would be if just ten percent of us would go in peace to love and serve the Lord and live the Truth. Even better, what if there was a reason to do so? What if the values of the Truth became the focus of the teachings and practices of all the religious faiths of the world?

The Truth is universal, consistent, basic, pure, and uncomplicated. The values of the Truth instruct us how to live. It is up to each of us to become aware of the Truth from within our souls, and to live what we know to be true. When we live from within our souls and live what matters, life becomes satisfying and meaningful. It is up to us to live the reason we are here, individually and collectively, and change our lives and the world for the betterment of mankind.

Background

Writing this book has been an experience of learning and growth that has been humbling, fulfilling, and amazing. I have been inspired and directed to deliver God's message of the Truth that is stated within this text. I do not consider myself the author, but the messenger presenting the information. This is a gift I have been given, and I know that I am to pass it on.

Writing a book is not something I ever thought I would do. The force to write this message was so incredibly strong I could not deny it. Throughout the process, it was important to me for the message to remain in its pure form. I did not discuss the contents with anyone until the book was completed. I did not want any outside influences involved, and this was in keeping with the guidance I was receiving.

The text is as I received it. The message of this text is actually simple and basic, but the message may appear unrealistic and even an impractical way to live life. This is only because of the views of our egos, and how far away from the Truth our lives have become.

I am not a religious person, and I am not a member of a religious organization. I have always had a deep faith in God and my allegiance is to God and his message of the Truth. The awareness of what I have known to be true has been with me since around age three. I was raised Catholic.

As a small child, I knew God and Jesus loved me and all people. I did not understand many of the rules of the Church, and did not believe the negative things I heard about God. What I knew about God was good and I could not see it any other way. I stayed in my own world ignoring the negativity. It was the second day of first grade when it all fell apart for me.

As a child, I expected Catholic school to be special. As Catholics, we were taught that we were closer to God than others, and we would get to go to heaven first when the world ended. On the second day, there was a group of four boys on the playground, who were being bullies and knocking kids down. I ended up being one of the kids knocked down. The moment I fell, everything I knew to be true became valid. I started crying and couldn't stop.

I continued to sob when we went back to class. The school called my parents to come and get me. They thought I was upset about starting school and being away from home. My tears were not from being away from home. My tears were because everything became so clear to me. I wanted so badly for the Church to be what I knew God's message to be. I realized as Catholics, we were not special or any different from the rest of the people on the earth. I did not understand why the Church presented contradictions about God's love, and knew I did not believe them. I knew God was good and loving, and what I felt about God's love was true.

After that day, I continued on, knowing I could not say what I felt or ask questions. My family did not discuss the church, we just seemed to function within the basic guidelines. The priest and nuns were much to intimidating, and I feared rejection for my thoughts. So, I simply ignored what I knew not to be true and continued on in my own world. Things went along smoothly until in second grade when we had to learn the Ten Commandments. This to me was another betrayal of God's message. Not that I did not and do not believe that they are good and valuable rules, but there were contradictions in the teachings.

Then the next thing was making my first Confession. I did not understand why I could not just talk to God and Jesus myself. I did not like that I had to make up sins to have something to say. After I made my first Confession, I did not want to ever go again. After leaving the confessional and saying my penance, I had a long talk with Jesus. I apologized for making up the sins I told the priest. I decided I would only tell my sins to Jesus when I needed to and not go to confession again. After third grade, I attended public schools.

I attended mass every Sunday with my family until I left for college. I took catechism classes through junior high. I respect the Catholic faith as I do all faiths. I do not feel my experiences would have been any different if my family had been part of any other faith at that time, and I am thankful for what the experience taught me.

I have always had strong feelings and beliefs about God, and hold what I know to be true in high regard, yet I have always lived my spiritual life in my own private world. It was not until one day in 1997, while listening to the radio on my way to a meeting, the focus of my spiritual life changed. There was an interview for a symposium being held that evening. Nick Bunick was discussing the book *The Messengers*, and he was going to speak. I knew immediately I had to attend the symposium. This was the first time anyone had made sense to me and confirmed what I knew to be true. About six months after the symposium, I decided to simplify my life and spend more quality time with my soul.

Early in 1999, God and Jesus spoke to me and told of their love. I was filled with the same love I had felt as small child. A few weeks later, I found myself wrapped in a blanket of love that was more intense and fulfilling than anything I had felt before. Words cannot describe the level of love and comfort.

(This feeling has remained with me and is a constant part of my life).

Over the next several years, my thoughts, wants, and needs started to change. I then found myself at a crossroad. I knew I no longer wanted to continue living the life I was living. A good life, earning a good living, fulfilled materially, but pointless.

Then 9/11/2001 occurred and my work came to a standstill. I took advantage of the time to continue to explore my soul. By the time January came, the thought of returning to work was not appealing. The connection to God, Jesus, and my soul had become stronger, and I loved the space I was in. By summer, information was pouring through me. In October (this is when I drove into the city described in the first chapter), I knew I was going to be writing the messages I was receiving. The guidance was strong, but I was unsure of me. Who was I to be writing this message directed by God and Jesus. It took me until January 2003 to become comfortable with the idea. The guidance to write was so strong that I allowed it to direct me without question. I would awaken early in the morning, usually around 2:30, bright and alert, with the information pouring from me and I would write whatever I was receiving.

The information came in various parts. In mid-March I organized my notes and began to type. As I typed, more information came to me. The text had a life of its own. When I went back and read what was on paper, I was amazed, remembering few of the details. I became overwhelmed with the information I was receiving, so I stopped mid-April to take stock of my thoughts.

I realized I was holding back some of the information I was receiving. I was concerned with what people would think. Looking for guidance, I made an appointment with Julia Ingram, coauthor of *The Messengers*, for what I described to her as enhancement for my life. The session was more than I expected. The identity of my soul was revealed to me.

In the session with Julia, I took myself back to a time two thousand years ago. It was revealed to me that I was Mary Magdalene during that time, and I carry a part of her soul now. I found myself in the most comfortable and familiar space I had ever been in. I have never felt so complete and whole. The love I felt, during the session, was the same love I had been feeling since 1999, but with an even stronger connection. My life, for the first time, made sense to me.

I returned home and remained in the state of the session, not wanting to be anywhere else. I did not start working on the book for about two weeks. During the session, Jeshua told me to carry on his message. I knew I was to do this, but I needed to know, "Why me?" When I asked, Jeshua smiled and said, "Because you know my love." During the session Julia asked, "Why was I to carry on the message?" He said, "People are tired, and they hunger to find life's meaning."

The focus and message of this book is the Truth as it applies to our lives. Up to this point, the Truth was written as pages of generalities. When I went back to working on the book, the Truth transformed into two chapters of specifics. During this time, I questioned if I need to be that specific. Jeshua said, "How else are they going to know unless we tell them. They will realize how simple it is when they hear it."

The experience of writing this text continued to amaze me. It was early in the morning on June 30 that I realized the importance of the Truth as it relates to learning life's lessons. I immediately went back through what was written and was amazed to find the information already there. This occurred again at the end of September, when I realized the further meaning of the message was the reason we are here.

I know all my life experiences up to this point were necessary to prepare me for this part of my life. My life, like all of our lives, is about learning and growth, and I am continuing to learn daily. I have had many spiritual experiences throughout my life, but none as profound and humbling as what I have experienced the last several years. The messages I had been receiving were what I already knew to be true, but the depth, meaning, and profound effect on my life was unexpected. I found myself in familiar yet uncharted territory. I knew I could not contain what I had been receiving, and I know that I am to deliver this message.

The message of God's Truth contained in this text is what each of us already knows within our souls. God's message was not meant to be complicated, and it is in its simplicity that we have become lost. The message is simple. It is simply "love."

It is my hope in reading this text you will become inspired to change your life, even if only a little. You may not agree with every word, but I hope you are inspired to go within, become conscious, connected with your soul, and live your life embracing the journey.

Mary McGovern